Praise for *Writing Alone Together*

"Part collaborative memoir, part self-help, this book in three voices offers seasoned guidance and structure to start and sustain a shared-leadership women's writing group, particularly for those new to journal writing and/or support circles. The authors' pure love of writing for creative self-expression, and for the power of writing in community, shines through on every page."

—Kathleen Adams, LPC, CEO, Center for Journal Therapy, Inc., author of *Journal to the Self* and editor of *Expressive Writing: Foundations of Practice*

"*Writing Alone Together* is both a culmination and a beginning. Through seven years of collaboration, Wendy, Lynda and Ahava have generously and joyfully produced a book to spark and support other women who seek to create journalling circles—to write their lives together."

—Judith Arcana, author of several books, including a biography of Grace Paley, and a member of "Jane" an abortion service in the seventies in Chicago

"*Writing Alone Together* is a beautiful book that encourages, inspires, and guides writers to create their own journaling communities. Through their shared experiences, prompts, and wisdom, Lynda, Wendy, and Ahava show that writing is far from a solitary act—rather, it's one that we can use not only to learn more about ourselves but also to deepen our connection to others."

—Hannah Braime, coach and founder of Becoming Who You Are

"I wholeheartedly recommend *Writing Alone Together*. My own journal experience started in much the same way that Wendy, Lynda and Ahava present here. Sharing my newly begun personal journal with a close friend who was open and supportive gave me the encourage-

D1555789

ment I needed. Soon I found my two careers in art and child development morphing into the new field of Art Therapy, specializing in Creative Journal groups in our community. That was 1976. As a pioneer in journal groups, I can vouch for this book. It not only guides the reader in how to organize and structure a group using powerful journal prompts, but reveals the texture, sound and feeling of real women working and growing together, telling their stories. Brava! A much needed book."

—Lucia Capacchione, Ph.D., A.T.R., R.E.A.T., art therapist and author of *The Creative Journal: The Art of Finding Yourself* and *The Power of Your Other Hand*

"*Writing Alone Together* is both inspirational and practical, offering a wealth of advice for any woman who wants to journal or be part of a journal writing group. The book will serve the growing need of women who wish to express themselves and create a new culture of open communication during these transformative times."

—Lorraine Gane, author of *The Way the Light Enters*, *The Blue Halo* and other books of poetry and prose

"These writers know—instinctively and from much experience—what scientists are just now discovering: That no matter the public reach of a work, the act of expressive writing is both healing and invigorating. In its most vital form, our storytelling becomes a practice at once personal, political, and communal. Take this book's invitation."

—Ariel Gore, founding editor of *Hip Mama* and author of *The End of Eve*

"*Writing Alone Together: Journalling in a Circle of Women for Creativity, Compassion and Connection* is fired in the heart's sacred and wild wisdom. Wendy Judith Cutler, Lynda Monk, and Ahava Shira have been writing a long time, alone and together. Based on their long life practices of journal writing, they offer us rare gifts of testimony, insight, courage, and encouragement. By weaving their distinct voices in a creative composition of stories, poetry, writing prompts, pedagogical insights, quotations, and ruminations, they call out a hopeful vision for transforming the world by attending to the energy of language for translating and transfusing our being and becoming as people in relationship with one another and with the whole of creation. This book bears witness to the compelling possibilities of nurturing wellness and sustainability in individual and communal lives by learning to communicate with ourselves and with one another."

—Carl Leggo, poet and professor at The University of British Columbia, Vancouver, Canada and editor of *A Heart of Wisdom: Life Writing as Empathetic Inquiry*

"What a valuable book! *Writing Alone Together* records and makes available to all the egalitarian, collective structure and process of women's journaling groups. It tells how to form a leaderless group and illustrates how to sustain a journal circle, so that each member is valued and nurtured towards fulfilling her individual voice and story. As a piece of writing itself, *Writing Alone Together* is a triumph of collective composition, the creation of three authors blended into a unified voice, at once lucid, wise and inspiring."

—Tristine Rainer, author of *The New Diary: How to Use a Journal for Self-Guidance and Expanded Creativity* and *Your Life as Story: Writing the New Autobiography*

"It's rare to be taken inside the experience of what is required of us as writers. In *Writing Alone Together*, Wendy Judith Cutler, Lynda Monk and Ahava Shira track how devotion and collaboration combust with alone and together to fuel us."

—Betsy Warland, author of *Breathing the Page: Reading the Act of Writing*

WRITING ALONE TOGETHER

Journalling in a Circle of Women
for Creativity, Compassion
and Connection

Wendy Judith Cutler, MA
Lynda Monk, MSW, RSW, CPCC
Ahava Shira, PhD

Butterfly Press
Salt Spring Island, BC

Library and Archives Canada Cataloguing in Publication

Cutler, Wendy Judith, 1952-, author
   Writing alone together : journalling in a circle of women for creativity, compassion and connection / Wendy Judith Cutler, Lynda Monk, Ahava Shira.
Includes bibliographical references.
Issued in print and electronic formats.
ISBN 978-0-9684619-2-1 (pbk.).--ISBN 978-0-9684619-3-8 (pdf)

   1. Creative writing--Therapeutic use. 2. Diaries--Authorship--Therapeutic use.
I. Monk, Lynda, -1969, author II. Shira, Ahava, -1967, author III. Title.

PN4390.C87 2014   808.06'692   C2014-906162-5
                                                   C2014-906163-3

Edited by Lorraine Gane
Designed by Mark Hand
Cover Photo by Shari MacDonald
Back Cover Photo by Ahava Shira
Authors' Photos by Peter Allan and Billie Woods
Butterfly Design by Jerry P. Longboat

Printed by Printorium Bookworks
Victoria, British Columbia

Butterfly Press is dedicated to "Metaphormosis"—the transformative power of writing to heal and expand our experience of life.

Disclaimer: While this book offers some of the healing and personal growth benefits of journalling and expressive writing, it is not meant to be a substitute for psychological counselling or medical care.

www.writingalonetogether.com

DEDICATIONS

WENDY

Always and forever, to my lovergirl, Corrie Hope Furst, who first gave me *The New Diary*, encouraged me to teach women's journal writing workshops and has listened to my words for over twenty-eight years, with whom I share my heart, my love, my life.

LYNDA

To my loving husband Pedro, who always encourages my voice in the world. And to our precious sons, Jackson and Jesse, who keep asking me, "Mommy, are you writing a real book?" I am honoured to share daily life amidst my *circle of boys.*

AHAVA

For Gregory, the lover of my dreams and visions, joys and possibilities, who makes my most cherished desires realizable with his nurturing presence and generous support.

Contents

Part One:

Writing Alone Together

In the privacy of our own
thoughts, dreams, desires
in living rooms,
kitchens, cafes, circles

we bring what is typically regarded
as personal experience
into community.

—Wendy

Our Invitation

What you hold in your hands is an invitation to experience journal writing as a communal practice for creativity, compassion and connection. Unlike most books about writing in a group, this is not a book that teaches how to critique one another's writing. Instead, it offers a process for sharing, listening and paying attention to our own and each other's lives, transforming writing into a catalyst for meaningful conversation, storytelling, mindfulness, personal growth, creative self-expression and mutual support. Part memoir, part writing practice, part inspiration, this book is a multi-voiced creation of three passionate and committed journal writers. We offer our journal entries written in and out of the margins, often messy and uncalculated, open and vulnerable, revealing the depth and complexity of experience that emerges from going to the blank page.

Throughout this book, we explore how we journal, what we journal about and how our journal writing has helped shape who we are personally, culturally, politically and spiritually. We show you how to cultivate this practice in your life: through prompts and exercises, quotations from women writers, our personal journal entries and suggestions for creating your own circles of women writing together. Woven throughout this book are universal themes we discovered through our writing and being together such as intimacy, creativity, sexuality, mothering, coming-out, work, family, friendships and relationships.

At the heart of this book is our belief that Writing Alone Together changes lives and, consequently, the world. This is our story: a weave of three women in words, journalling alone and together for the joy, pleasure and sanity of it. This is how we cope, how we celebrate, how we learn, how we listen, how we play.

We invite you into this conversation with ourselves on the page, ourselves and the world, ourselves and our lives. We encourage you to bask in the brilliance of your own words and those of other women, to honour all of your truths, to acknowledge your courage and to open your heart as you write for yourself and with others.

What is Writing Alone Together?

Writing Alone Together is a practice of gathering with other women to write, read and create a sense of community through the transformational power of journal writing. This communal practice creates shifts in consciousness, in our lives and in the world. Each time we meet, we bring the intention of being fully present, listening to ourselves and to one another and sharing our words, thoughts, views, visions, dreams and intuition. While we may not always agree or feel resonance with one another's ideas or experiences, through Writing Alone Together we cultivate acceptance and compassion.

Through writing in journals, we discover and re-member the stories and poetry of our lives. As we share and reveal these stories within these pages and within our journalling circle, we begin to see new perspectives, gain clarity, find solutions, celebrate accomplishments, notice and change patterns of be-haviour and refine our understanding of our life ex-periences. In this process, we make meaning through our stories, constructing who we are and who we are becoming.

To write is, above all else, to construct a self... Journal entries and life histories, as well as fictions, poems, and plays, are variations on the most fundamental human need to know oneself deeply and in relationship to the world.

—DEENA METZGER

Writing Alone Together deepens our connections to ourselves and creates a sense of community with other women. Being part of a circle transforms our sense of isolation and separateness into a grounded awareness of our interconnectedness and universal consciousness. As we become familiar with the ways we connect with one another, we sense the synergy between our individual lives and the larger world we inhabit. We learn to recognize our strengths and resources, our internal censors and judges and the thoughts and self-perceptions that limit us and hold us back from expressing our full potential. We also deepen our appreciation for the fullness of others and what they bring to the circle.

Writing Alone Together is a practice that teaches us about self-love and acceptance, bringing us into deeper compassion and care with and for one another. Through journal writing together and sharing our words and stories, we learn how to honour differences. We discover that witnessing one of us express herself gives each of us permission to honour our truths more fully.

When we come together—to write, to read, to listen, to witness—we are living our creativity. We acknowledge ourselves as creative beings. Each time we meet with the intention of expressing our authentic selves, we claim our creativity.

Writing is not simply self-expression. Writing is a way to seek lines of connection and intersection with others, to compose creative and lively possibilities for living stories, for making up stories, for revising stories, for turning stories inside out and upside down so they are always transforming and transformative.

—ERICA HASEBE-LUDT, CYNTHIA M. CHAMBERS AND CARL LEGGO

In North American culture that emphasizes individualism, separatism and hierarchies of power, bringing our bodies, words and stories together in the same room is significant. Coming together as equals with mutual respect is radical. Over time, Writing Alone Together creates a structure that transforms who we are individually and collectively. As women, we need ways of coming together to collaborate, heal and evolve. With this practice we bring healing to the world. This is the essence of belonging.

Wendy Writes...

When we are in touch with our selves—our thoughts, our feelings, our perceptions, our dreams—then we have the potential to create change in our lives and in the larger world we inhabit. Imagine if we lived in a world in which all or even most of us were aware of our real needs and desires, and expressed this to one another. Our world would have to change. People wouldn't be able to accept actions or behaviours that they don't support.

When we feel that we are part of the world, we feel empowered and more hopeful. We are able to connect with others and feel part of a community. Acknowledging these connections creates the energies that move us towards living more conscious lives.

Writing Alone Together is the sacred, creative work of personal and collective storytelling. The heart and art of writing and telling stories have been used for millennia in cultures around the world as ways of learning, teaching, caring, sharing, connecting and creating community. When we write we tell the stories of our lives—the dark and light, the struggles and successes, the hopes and fears, the aches and pleasures. We are curious about how our stories shape us and how they constrain us. We help one another become open to the continually shifting nature of our stories. We write our stories to learn about ourselves, to enlarge our understanding of ourselves and one another. We write to heal, we write to grow. Journalling helps us stay grounded in the story we want to live.

Ahava Writes...

We breathe on the page, writing like breathing, making our living known here, rehearsing our stories, rehearing those we have told before, remembering old lines and summoning new ones. What if I/we told it this way? Writing Alone Together is a story-creating and story-telling practice that enriches our lives. We learn to re-write old stories that have become stifling or unsympathetic to us. Through writing our lives as stories, we learn to recognize and acknowledge the universal elements of our personal experience. As we write, we expand. We ask unexpected questions about the meaning of life, find answers and awaken new ways of thinking. Every time we write and reflect, we are in the act of becoming more aware. Writing teaches us how to be in our lives differently, to be more awake.

Who This Book is For

This book is for women who are seeking a way to experience change or deeper reflection, whether as solitary writers or as part of a women's writing community. This book is also for you if:

- You write, have written or have wanted to write.

- You have journalled but have never read or shown anything you've written to anyone else.

- You are curious about what it might be like to share your journal writing with others.

- You have always wanted to meet and write with other women, but weren't sure how to begin.

- You have been told by your therapist, counsellor, teacher, doctor, coach, friend or support group that you should keep a journal.

- You want inspiration, support and time for regular writing practice.

- You already belong to a writer's group and want affirmation and ideas for deepening your experience together.

- You want to remember what matters to you.

- You want to be present, awake, grateful for your life.

Everybody is talented, original and has something important to say.

—BRENDA UELAND

How This Book Came to Be

This book has lived alongside our lives for seven years, testing our resolve, teasing out our differences, questioning our commitments, lifting our hearts and grounding us in our ever-changing lives. Our hundred years of combined journal writing experience informs our process, practice and passion for Writing Alone Together.

As we conceived of and committed to this project, our meetings shifted from journal writing together into co-authoring this book. At times, we missed the ease we had felt when journalling; however, this new project took on a life of its own and we felt gratitude and excitement for our creative collaboration.

We take you into our pause, the moment we asked ourselves: What have we been doing here—this coming together to journal? Why are we doing this? What benefits are coming from this practice? Is it possible other women might benefit from doing this, too? Is it possible journalling can be so transformative that there might be even deeper benefits by doing this with others in a group? How have our lives been transformed by this decision to do this collaboratively? What is possible within this time of reflection? What exactly happens when reading our journals aloud to one another? This book takes you into our efforts to answer these questions, both for ourselves and for you.

Lynda Writes...

As a social worker, I was trained in a model of understanding whereby what affects the individual impacts the whole and what impacts the whole influences the individual. It is not enough to assume, as we so often do in our self-driven culture, that indi-

vidual transformation will lead to collective change. Writing Alone Together offers the chance for transformation and growth at the individual and collective levels. It invites us to explore questions and learn how to be with the unknown parts of our selves, the unknown parts of our lives. The capacity to be with the unknown is one of the keys to all transformation.

How to Use this Book

Writing Alone Together consists of a series of Practices, Principles, Prompts and Personal Journal Entries. You might start with the four practices or dive into the principles. You may play with the prompts or be drawn into our personal journal entries.

We offer you these as suggestions, invitations and inspirations. Feel free to explore, experiment and discover what works best for you and your circle of women. Based on the skills you each bring, what matters to you and the issues you face, your circle will be unique.

Journalling Prompts and Writing

Write fast, write everything, include everything, write from your feelings, write from your body, accept whatever comes.

—TRISTINE RAINER

Throughout the book, we've included writing prompts to inspire, encourage and support your journal writing practice. Writing prompts can be words, phrases, statements, sentence starters, quotes and questions which lead you to the page and deepen your process of discovery when you are there.

There is no right or wrong way to respond to writing prompts, individually or as a circle. Whatever you write is right. Your writing may be as long or as short as you want. You may consider timing your writing for five, ten, fifteen or thirty minutes, or you may choose to keep going until you feel you've come to an end and have nothing more to write. You might even go past that, and write beyond where you wanted to stop, to learn what's on the other side.

We also encourage you to discover your own ways onto the page. Try starting your writing with whatever is in front of you: a feeling, thought, image, line from a book you are reading, words you overheard on the bus or your impression of the view outside your window. Anything that inspires you and helps you enter into writing can be considered a prompt.

However you choose to engage with the contents of these pages, may they spark curiosity, creativity, connection and compassion within as you journey from inside the journal to sharing your words with others.

Ahava Writes...

Your journal writing circle can become a refuge, companion, touchstone, confidante, a place of peace and of acceptance, where you can feel grounded as life pulls you in a hundred directions. Try it yourself. You will see, it will feel like home, this circle of women who write alone together. It will feel like home.

Part Two:

Weave of Three

We are three women on the edge of the circle.
We stand here and hold the thread of the heavens
in one hand, the needle of the earth in the other.

We weave them into stories,
making it whole again over and over with each telling.

We weave stories for birth and stories for dying, stories
for betrayal and for reunion, stories for all the joys and
sorrows of our lives.

And we leave room for those stories yet to be told.

—Ahava

Journal Writing Journeys

When we come together and share our stories, it expands our notion of what is possible. It changes the person telling the story, it changes whoever is listening to the story, and it changes how we understand our own story.

—Ai-Jen Pod

Here we share our individual journal writing journeys. You will read about how Lynda used journal writing to prevent burnout as a young social worker; how Wendy used it to claim her identity as a lesbian and a feminist; and how Ahava's poems, stories and philosophy of Loving Inquiry first showed themselves in the pages of her journal. Then we offer our first encounter as a circle of three, what we were feeling leading up to that moment and how we fell into comfort with journalling together. Next you will be introduced to the essential elements for creating a journal writing circle of your own.

To become more acquainted with our individual experiences with journal writing, we responded to the following prompt:

Journal Writing Prompt   **What is your experience with journal writing? Tell the story of your journal writing journey.**

LYNDA

I don't remember how old I was when I first started putting words on paper for pleasure and storytelling. Was I printing or writing? Did I pause to check for spelling or just free fall onto the page with no teacher's voice correcting me along the way? Did I tell anyone of this writing obsession or was it a secret? I can see my Nancy Drew books on the shelf above my desk so perhaps it was all very mysterious. Eventually, I surrendered the key on my journal and the book grew bigger with larger pages, thicker spines, artistic covers, some lined, some blank sheets, coils, spines, the pens were blue, green, purple, then a stint in pencil just in case I had to erase my words leaving no trace of my inner world, thoughts and feelings to be found by another.

I don't remember starting to write and I don't remember stopping. I don't remember if I picked up a cigarette or dipped back to the page first. I remember writing in my journal, drinking coffee—regular, one cream, one sugar—and long inhales on Du Maurier lights, king size. The paper stained with java and jealousy and mistakes. In university I was wrapped in deadlines, books, papers and learning, often loving my affair with my journal more than discussions of anti-oppressive social work practice and neo-liberalism and the hungry hippo, explorations of Canada's poor. At that time I was prolific in projects, graded for my ideas and compassion and thoughtful analysis of social problems and human suffering, my opinions were cultivated in my observation of the world around me, all watched through the lens of my pen moving over paper in my journal. I can hear the scratch of my .5 mm Pilot pen marking the twenty pound sketch pad inking ideals into essays and presentations.

I wrote and I wrote in my early years as a social worker within child welfare. At midnight, four in the morning, after getting home from an emergency child abuse investigation, I would write with the smell of smoke, blood and lost innocence on my fingertips, in my skin. Hardships, violations, rape, dead babies, battered little boys, traumatized girls, sometimes picking them up in their pajamas and terror to drive them to a stranger's house in the middle of the night. I would not go home right away, knew I could not sleep. I would find an all night coffee shop and I would write and smoke and my tears would mix with ink and my night's experience turned into words and blur and moments I would try to forget and always remember.

I did not know about vicarious trauma as a twenty-two-year-old social worker. I had no warning in all those university classes that beyond the ecological model of social work practice and neat theories of human development and Paulo Freire's *Politics of Oppression,* that all of this would have a smell and a bitterness that I would taste with each swallow, or that I would wake in the night cold with sweat, or feel my heart race when I saw naked skin with bruises and cuts when a four-year-old girl had to pull her pants down and show me where Daddy had hit her with his belt. We didn't talk about this at staff meetings or in supervision. We reported statistics and case notes and recorded the facts for court. Every now and then black humour and a chuckle filled the staff room, the sounds always feeling broken and cracked to me, less like human laughter and more like the cry of a caged animal. Victims and helpers all in steel-sided circumstances, together with no place to go except towards whatever ray of hope and innocence might be seen from the outside looking in, or the inside looking out. Either way, always on the wrong side of something, even rightness.

I filled journal after journal after journal of the stories we did not speak. I wrote in the parking lot, sitting in my car, after the funeral of a thirteen-year-old boy who hanged himself in his family garage after the last class of the day. I wrote deep into and out the other side of all this pain and suffering, his and mine. I did not know it then, but I was writing to keep myself whole, sane and observant of life bigger than all this blackness. I was writing to find and celebrate resiliency, mine and others'. I was writing to construct meaning out of the most meaningless tragedies. I was writing to hold perspective, to stay in touch with optimism. Writing allowed me to keep breathing when I was holding my breath for too long. Writing held me up, sat me down, kept me believing in the power of the human spirit. It still does.

I have written on beach chairs over white sand in Hawaii, put words on pages during marriage, divorce, pregnancy and miscarriages. I have moved my mind and my life across miles and experiences creating myself word by word, reflecting on joy, love, loss, hope, marvelling at what I remember and what I forget. I have written while students in my vicarious trauma workshops have done their own reflecting. I facilitate and I pause and I write while they get coffee on their breaks, or work in small groups on an exercise. I write.

During labour, while I breathed into my lower back, trying to visualize my hips widening, I wrote from my mind to my body preparing my womb to release my first-born son. I sat on a big purple birthing ball, leaned over to the mattress of my hospital bed and used it as my desk as I wrote before and after contractions. I poured pure love onto the pages with my newborn son cradled in my arms.

When I wake in the morning and fold into my husband's arms, my mind wanders to my journal on our nightstand. I kiss him and he rises to make our morning coffee and I reach for my paper and pen, begin by putting words, lists, poems, ideas, longings and gratitude on the page, this space where I live and love and learn.

My journal is a sacred space—it is where I give birth to myself and my life over and over again. This practice of journal writing is at once an extension and the core of who I am as a woman. I know I would be someone different, less here in this world without it. With it, I embrace all that is—as I know it and don't know it in this one moment—while all these other moments of my life stack up behind me, layered like rose petals, soft and held up by a strong, spiky stem of lived experience. In this life, with the blank page and full presence, I am complete.

WENDY

I found you when I was ten. Baby blue, with a drawing of a girl with a ponytail. A perfect gift for me, who longed to write my life. I felt compelled to put words down on paper. I filled up this and a few other diaries with keys and locks and also kept a scrapbook filled mostly with playbills of my ballet performances and other memorabilia collected from ballet and birthday celebrations and some school activities. I've often thought I was a scribe in a past life. The compulsion to record everything feels ancient, like an action I've repeated over and over, from time immemorial.

In college in Berkeley in 1970, I transitioned into binders and the writing in my diaries connected to notes from college courses, books I was reading and even poems I composed. It was a turbulent time of fervent student protests against the war in Vietnam and a flurry of organized movements and actions.

As usual, the diary kept me grounded in a time of frenzied flux and transition. It felt vibrant to be exposed to so much radical thought and action. The streets were teeming with an explosion of activities: the air filled with incense, marijuana, patchouli oil and sometimes the lingering scent of tear gas from the previous riots, Telegraph Avenue lined with craftspeople selling their wares, Black Panthers selling their newspapers, poets hawking their poetry books and sometimes reading poems aloud on the street corners, politicos announcing the next demonstration or rally, Hare Krishnas clanging their bells and dancing down the aisles of the streets and folks of all shapes and colours and ideologies and scents, including dogs, lots of dogs, mostly unleashed. I felt alive in a way I had never been, that my life was taking shape in exciting and glorious ways, and that anything could happen. The diary provided safety and constancy. I almost never felt alone.

It wasn't until my second year of college that I began to keep a "journal." This foray into journal writing coincided with having transported myself across the country to attend a small, liberal arts, extremely progressive, experimental and experiential college in Vermont (Goddard College). There I immersed myself in Anaïs Nin's diaries (who actually visited and gave a reading there) and Simone de Beauvoir's memoirs. I devoured these and other books by and about women which prompted me to keep my own journal. I began to experience such freedom that I had never known.

I enrolled in a feminist history course and began identifying as a feminist. I experimented with smoking marijuana, which I found to be fascinating, mind-enhancing and freeing. And I started being sexual and sharing my sexuality with men/boys. This all provided me with endless, energetic, explorative and intense journal writing. Actually I became quite obsessive about these entries. I would become distressed with myself if I failed to make an entry each day. I also guarded my privacy and maintained that it was up to me if I wanted to share or not, considering it sacred and private. This privacy allowed me the safety to write as uncensored as I could.

Since then, I have never been without a journal. I used to carry it with me everywhere I went. Especially when I visited my parents' house, I would make certain it was in my backpack whenever I left the house, terrified of the thought of my mother ever getting her hands on it. As her eyesight worsened and she found difficulty reading, this fear relaxed.

I felt lured to return to Berkeley. I soon became a member of a feminist collective "Bay Area Women Against Rape." The collective provided rape counselling, anti-sexist education and engaged in feminist process including endless meetings, which were time-consuming, but which I loved. My role as scribe came in handy as I endlessly scribbled down notes of everything that transpired.

My journal soon integrated records of meetings, notes for speaking engagements, drafts of statements and position papers, summaries of books I read, class notes of lectures and discussions, panels, forums, clippings from newspapers and newsletters, letters and drafts of letters, ideas for benefits and events—as well as other personal musings, including crushes and attractions, relationships, heartbreaks, desires, losses, struggles and all things feminist and political and questioning of existing structures of society. All of this found its place in my journals.

Now thoroughly immersed in feminist community and collective projects, I began to meet women who identified themselves as lesbians. Lesbian feminism became a visible force in the women's movement. A renaissance for lesbians was emerging in the 1970s such as was never before possible. Herstory was most certainly being created.

Acknowledging and following my impulses, my instincts, my desires as I scribbled them within the pages of my journal, I found myself falling in love with my best friend. Sandra and I became lovers. My journal contained the drafts of my coming-out letter to my parents. It was something I felt compelled to do in response to my mother's regular pleas about whether I was dating men and, if I wasn't, why wasn't I. She was never to accept me as her lesbian daughter. I also sent the letter to the local lesbian newspaper (*Rubyfruit Reader*), a national lesbian newsletter (*Lesbian Connection*) and the editors of a coming-out anthology. It was published in the first two publications and accepted for publication in the anthology, except the first press dissolved (Daughters) and the next press was the target of arson (Diana Press). It was later published by Persephone Press *(The Coming Out Stories)*, a full four years after that. My parents never knew that it had been published anywhere. Putting it out there like that, for others to read, somewhat helped to lessen the bitter rejection from my parents. I knew that I was not alone.

I continued to use my journal for multiple purposes—for classes, political action and personal reflection, recollection, revelation. I moved to Santa Cruz to begin an interdisciplinary PhD graduate school program with a concentration on feminism and radical politics. I began teaching, first as a teaching assistant, then as a co-teacher with a collective of women and later as an instructor of my own writing courses, finding that I loved creating an environment where writing was the primary focus. I always used journal writing exercises with my students which seemed to allow them to be more connected with their own feelings and to more

openly share with others. That moment when the silence of the room is only interrupted by the sounds of
pens and pencils moving on paper is a true delight for
me and never fails to move me.

I've journeyed along the West Coast, first in California, then Oregon and now on this magical island
in British Columbia that I call home with my lovergirl
and life partner, Corrie. I have kept writing, no matter what—first as a young, activist, radical teacher of
writing, then a women's studies instructor and now a
facilitator of women's writing circles. Writing has become my way of making sense of my life. With my
journal and a favourite pen in my bag, I can weather
any heart-break, organize thoughts, open my eyes and
body and mind and heart and imagine anything.

AHAVA

I bought my first journal in Montreal. I was twenty
years old and on my way to Europe for three-and-a-
half-months backpacking by myself. No family, no one
telling me when to come home nor what to eat nor
where to spend my money. I was preparing for heaven.
So I went with a journal and an open mind.

I wrote in point form to start, then after a while
came fuller sentences about what I was seeing as I
roamed from town to town, the train rides and the
people I was meeting, the challenges I was facing in
the relationships between them and the feelings I was
having about visiting all the new places.

The next journal accompanied me on my second
journey away from home, this time to Israel for a year
of study, only a few months after the first. This one still
has many blank pages for I stopped writing about mid-

way through the year. It was Jacob, my first real love, who had distracted me.

The third was started at home, prompted by the confusion from another relationship. That, and I was trying to decide which direction to take for a career. It was so difficult to choose. All my old friends seemed to have known where they were going after high school. Many were now in professional programs, moving steadily toward becoming lawyers, doctors, dentists and business people. In the journal I found a place to grapple with whether to become a social worker, study massage or pursue a more artistic life.

The next was written away from home again, in Big Sur, California. I had traveled to the oldest New Age retreat centre in North America for a winter of inner work. There I started to acknowledge and try to understand the emotional and physical trauma I had endured as an adolescent, and continued to consider my career path, nixing social work school for the potential of studying dance and the performing/healing arts at the Naropa Institute in Boulder, Colorado.

From that point on I have never not had a journal, whether writing poetry about family betrayal, the beauty of the natural world or chronicling the pleasures and frustrations from friendships and intimate relationships.

What have I been doing in my journals? I have been working toward writing a new story for my life, healing myself from past pain, the anxiety of adolescence, finding a new home, a physical place where I could lay my head and a home for my heart and soul and dreams, a place of peace where I could feel safe and loved for who I was (becoming), not for who others wanted me to be. That's what I've been writing about for over twenty years, this journey of movement from what other people wanted from me to what I truly want for myself and my own life.

My mother and I did not get along very well during much of my late adolescence. She had a strong sense of over-protectiveness and a need to control those around her. I wanted out, freedom, attention to my own desires and needs. No wonder I had to leave home to write in my journal the first few years. Then I left home for good, flying all the way across Canada to flee the constriction. I wanted to explore, to go places and see things and I wanted to meet new people and especially to find out what was in me. Of course I was scared. And I wrote that too in my journal, all about my fears and what stopped me from doing the things I wanted to do. I also wrote about my dreams, the plans I had to live on an island and love someone with whom I could be all of who I imagined I could be.

The words kept coming and it felt so good to be writing them down and then the poems came with the anger at the incest and the realization that this was not only a personal thing but it was because I was a woman and in our culture women were exploited in the media and abused by their spouses and partners and they earned less money than men who did the same job. I became furious and wanted to know more and grew passionate about empowering myself in as many ways as I could.

I wrote poem after poem in my journals and other ideas for creative pursuits. I started to write a play in my journal in 1995 that I finished in 1999 and together with my partner, staged and performed as a one-woman show. The journals became multifaceted: part psychological self-analysis, part creative muse, part travelogue, part relationship chronicle, part poetry handbook.

I've had my blue period, my red period, black period, pink period, seashells, butterflies, hard cover and soft cover, lined and unlined. I wrote in blue and black ink, with fountain pens in red and blue and black, with pencil. I wrote in restaurants, cafés, on buses, trains, in cars and on airplanes, and on long ferry rides through Active Pass. I wrote at home alone in bed, one of my favourite places to write.

I wrote in the solarium looking out toward the North Shore mountains on East 22nd and Main streets when I first lived in Vancouver; spread out on the pale green '70s shag carpet in the furniture-free living room on West 43rd Avenue in Kerrisdale; snuggled into the worn brown corduroy couch looking out at the ocean on Rainbow Road on Salt Spring Island; leaning against a pillow in my window seat on Orchard Road; and out on the back deck overlooking the Salish Sea on Seclusion Lane. I've lived in twenty homes during the past twenty years and have written several journals in every one.

Most recently, I have been writing on Butterstone Farm, my new and now permanent home on Salt Spring. Here I continue to write about relationships and love, although now I also write about gates and openings and a practice I teach called Loving Inquiry. I still write poems, like the one I penned yesterday about the quality of light coming through the window after the rain.

The journal has always been a story catcher, also a worry catcher, pattern catcher. A constant companion, through my journal I let the burdens of this life with all its demands and responsibilities rest. I find refuge there and joy and clarity, and especially a deep and abiding inner peace.

Journal Writing Prompt

The "journey" metaphor can be a useful way to review your previous journalling and to reflect on your life. Here are some entry points to write about your own "journal writing journey":

1. Where have you journeyed since beginning to write in your journal? What kind of journey has it been?

2. If you have never written in a journal, dream into it: What would you want your journal writing journey to be like?

3. Return to your first journal writing moment. Where were you when you first started to write? What got you started? What did your first journal look like? How old were you? What was going on in your life at the time?

4. Have you ever stopped journal writing? Why?

5. Have you ever shared your journal writing with someone else?

6. Have you ever written in community with other journal writers?

Coming Together: How We Embarked on this Journey

> *The diary is the only form of writing that encourages total freedom of expression. Because of its very private nature, it has remained immune to any formal rules of content, structure, or style. As a result the diary can come closest to reproducing how people really think and how consciousness evolves.*

—TRISTINE RAINER

AHAVA

I am a writer, poet and journal writer. I have been handwriting in notebooks for twenty-seven years. A few years ago I was perusing Salt Spring's community directory and came across an advertisement under the W's titled: WomenWriting Journal Workshop. It must be someone new to the island, I thought, as I had never seen the ad before. I wondered what kind of writing activities the woman would facilitate. I also wanted to know more about the woman herself. Who was she and what was her experience with journal writing? As a journal writer I am always curious when I hear or read about others who have chosen to participate in the same activity that I have been doing day after day, week after week, month after year after decade.

At about the same time that I saw the ad for journal writing workshops, I had decided to embark on a personal project to revisit my journals (about a hundred of them).

In my journal entry on July 9, 2006 I wrote:

> *I spread out all of my journals onto my porch. Slowly I started to arrange them in groups according to colour, size, shape. Next I displayed them in various spaces around the courtyard. Then I took photographs. I had never done this before. They had been sitting idle on the top shelf of my bedroom closet for years. How good it felt to take them out and move them around a bit, spend some time with them again. Some of them I hadn't held in nearly two decades.*

The air of synergistic coincidence made what I did next inevitable. I picked up the phone and dialled the number in the directory and began to have a conversation with Wendy, a woman who had recently moved to the island from Oregon and has been journal writing for more than thirty-seven years. We had an immediate connection. Not only did we share a passionate lifetime commitment to journalling, we both identified as Jewish women. We decided to get together and met a few days later at a local café. The first thing we chose to do together was write in our journals.

Wendy and I met two or three times during that summer. Each time, we got together to write at the same café in Ganges. We read each other our words, talked about our experiences with journalling, got to know each other through listening to each other's stories after we had shaped them on the page through writing. Holidays came and went and we missed several meetings. Toward the end of the summer Wendy led her first journal writing workshop on Salt Spring Island and I attended. Eight women gathered in a beautiful yurt to write and share our writing.

The fall came and went and neither of us was able to make any time to meet. We kept putting it off. The New Year came and went, too. On February 2, the Wiccan holiday of Candlemas, we were finally able to meet again. It was at that meeting I mentioned a friend of mine, another long-time journal writer. I was wondering if it would work for the three of us to get together. Wendy seemed interested, if a bit tentative. We had already established a sense of trust between us. I was nervous too, although I had an instinct that it would work to include my friend Lynda, a woman I had been very close with when I first moved to Salt Spring. The two of us had also spent some time together, writing and reading our words aloud to each other. We had drifted apart when our lives went in different directions. However, whenever we saw each other we reminded each other of it, and of how we hoped we could do it again.

On the first day the three of us met, things between us just clicked. It was amazing. We were all eager to write. We chose to write about our relationship to our writing selves. The three of us have been meeting for more than seven years now. We believe we have been creating something powerful and empowering that will have implications for our individual lives, for women's lives in our community and beyond, for all women's lives.

> *Writing was the healing place where I could collect bits and pieces, where I could put them together again…written words change us all and make us more than we could ever be without them.*

—BELL HOOKS

WENDY

First there was just me. Keeping journals. Keeping track. Pouring myself into these books, since I was nineteen and began reading the diaries of Anaïs Nin and Simone de Beauvoir's memoirs. Always writing, until there were stacks and stacks, rows upon rows of journals of all shapes and sizes, strewn all over my room.

Many years passed. Corrie and I had become lovers and she brought me to a magical campground in British Columbia. We continued to camp at the end of summer most every year and fantasized living there. Miraculously, after three years and two applications, we were granted permanent resident status in Canada.

We moved from Portland, Oregon to this beautiful island in this other country. I was craving community with other women, time to focus on my writing and to bring this together by facilitating workshops for women. So I put an ad in the local paper to teach a workshop and another in the island's community directory.

Ahava phoned me up and we decided to meet.

Then there were two of us. Thrilled to share our passion for journal writing with another (Jewish) woman. She had just taken photographs of her journals laid out in piles outside her house and brought these to our meeting. We wrote together on a table outside a café. She asked if we could invite her friend, a woman who had two young boys, to join us as she was another avid journal writer.

And then there were the three of us. The symmetry, the vibrations, the energies were palpable, as if we had been meeting like this for years. We knew many of the same books and authors, discovered familiarity and commonalities in our experiences with journal writing and to the ways it had sustained us in our lives.

Coming together in a journal writing circle with Ahava and Lynda felt natural to me, a kind of coming home—to ourselves, to the comfort of our written words and sharing with one another. We have become writing sisters, filling the pages of our own journals and of our book. I am so grateful for this opening and connecting, for the constancy we continue to manifest and our commitment to our beloved *Writing Alone Together.*

Writing is how I do 'it.' Writing is how I do everything. Writing is how I metabolize life. It is food for thought and it is food itself. If a difficult situation comes up in my life, I write at it as well as write about it.

—JULIA CAMERON

LYNDA

The fire warmed the room, the tea pot was covered with a quilted cozy, books, papers, journals and pens filled the space in Ahava's home. Jesse, my newborn son, only three weeks old, stirred in his carrier seat beside me while we introduced ourselves to one another. Here I was sitting in a circle, on the floor, with Ahava, always a soul sister since our first meeting years earlier while both working at the Salty Spring Spa as massage practitioners and healers, now here before me as a fellow writer and lover of words. Inside I was marvelling at how I missed sharing space and time with her over the past number of years while our lives were being lived in different directions. And Wendy, someone I had never met before, our first greeting, a hug, so easy, kind and familiar in some way. Our connection and chemistry, our group of three, was instant, the power of our shared love of words and journal writing creating a foundation for jumping into the mystery of our yet-to-be-defined new "writing group" together.

I was grateful to have a space, a small sliver of time to be my writer self, while navigating all the newness of my mother self. With two baby boys, my other son only eighteen months old at the time, now defining me and my role and identity in the world, I wanted to have a thread of space for my always-loved journalling practice. Somehow the validation of being with Ahava and Wendy, as writers, as journal writers, held a corner of my life and heart on the page, like trying to hold a kite being carried away by the wind. I needed this place of holding to keep giving myself permission and time to go to the page in the midst of it all. I appreciated being able to bring my sleep-deprived state and my baby boy to our early months of getting together to write. In other words, I could bring my whole self, the reality of my life in the moment, to our circle, to our time together, and I always felt in the exact right place, in the exact right time, with the exact right women. And I still do, after seven years of wondering and wandering together in our weave of words and womanhood.

I loved how we did not know where we were going, or exactly what we were doing together, that we all could say "yes" to form loosely held. With this spirit of curiosity, openness and love of writing and care for one another, our times together easily found a rhythm, process and deepened purpose. We always eat, check-in, share, write, read our writing, reflect and care. These are the bones of our origin story and the heart of our co-created path we now call *Writing Alone Together*.

Creating a Circle of Your Own

We are part of the circle. When we plant, when we weave, when we give birth, when we organize, when we heal, when we run through the park while the redwoods sweat mist, when we do what we're afraid to do, we are not separate. We are of the world and of each other, and the power within us is a great, if not an invincible power. Though we can be hurt, we can heal; within us is the power of renewal. And there is still time to choose that power.

—STARHAWK

Listening, witnessing, role modeling, reacting, deepening, mirroring, laughing, crying, grieving, drawing upon experience, and sharing the wisdom of experience, women in circles support each other.

—JEAN SHINODA BOLEN

We refer to the formation of coming together as a "circle." There are concrete reasons for this. By its nature, a circle is a structure that has no hierarchy. Within circles, the energies and interactions move among those present. Circles are important structures in sharing information, power and knowledge. They are ancient symbols and containers for practice, vital in feminist organizations, indigenous cultures and creative communities. Communing in a circle of women is what we do when we come together to write, to read, to listen, to witness.

Tips For Tending Your Own Circles

1. Commit to Meet Regularly

Determining a time and place for a first meeting is essential in setting the momentum and manifesting a beginning circle. Considerations include: where to meet (home, office, community centre, café), how often to meet (every week, once a month or even longer times in between), for how long (two to three hours, preferably) and how many women to include. Ways to find members can be as diverse as gathering some friends, putting up notices in your neighbourhood or posting online, making announcements at meetings and workplaces or just quietly inviting women you know to journal write together. Bringing women together who are willing to make and honour a commitment to meet regularly creates constancy and a foundation for the circle.

It is important to consider each woman's needs with regards to time constraints, privacy issues, family or child-caring needs and finances (if you must rent a space) when beginning. Be sure to address them with sensitivity and compassion. Not discussing these concerns can prevent a group from getting started.

As a circle, we have taken some leaves and stretches of time apart, to accommodate our separate needs and plans. Like any relationship or enduring friendship, we must decide over and over again to maintain our connection.

2. Negotiate the Structure of the Circle

Most often when people come together in a circle they expect there to be a leader, teacher or facilitator, someone who is responsible for how things go. Meeting without a designated leader, as is the case with Writing Alone Together, we create a structure to support this wherein each of us must develop and hone the skills necessary for the circle to function.

When we choose to be part of a leaderless (or "leaderful") structure, all of us, in a sense, become leaders with the responsibility of contributing to the circle's process and being responsible for creating a workable and nourishing structure. We also learn invaluable skills through recognizing our own resources and putting them into practice. Creating this kind of responsive and nurturing leadership necessitates that the responsibility be shared equally. This is reflective of feminist collective structures, which rely on the shared and equal participation of all members of the circle.

If we are not accustomed to doing this or have not done this for a long time, we may feel reluctant to offer ourselves as resources. Meanwhile, those of us who are comfortable may take on too much responsibility, sometimes to the detriment of our own well-being. It is a challenging balance and a totally worthwhile one to pursue. Being in relationship with one another in this way brings out what is within and among us.

Being in a leaderless circle doesn't mean there is never someone who leads or facilitates, but that the role of the facilitator is shared and rotated according to the needs and desires of individuals within the circles. Those who have experience with facilitation will be able to hone their skills and others who are unfamiliar will develop important skills. Sharing the leadership of a group is an important benefit of working together and reinforces that we are all leaders and followers.

The process of keeping the structure of a circle flowing can be one of the roles of the facilitator. This can be done by keeping track of what is occurring to both ensure that no one person dominates or disappears and also everyone has the opportunity to participate. In a less-structured format, each person takes responsibility for what transpires.

In our circle, we have alternated between having a designated facilitator and sometimes not having one. During some sessions, one of us has felt motivated to take the facilitator role. Other times, we intuitively moved into a topic which stemmed from something that was shared during our check-in.

3. Open the Circle by Checking-In

Opening each circle can happen in a variety of ways: You can start with a moment of silence or enact a short ritual for creating the energetic sacred container that holds the circle during your time together. This can consist of each woman taking a bit of time to share how she feels in the present and what's happening of significance with her writing and in her regular life. You can pre-determine the amount of time you want to take for this—usually five to ten minutes is enough, although sometimes more is needed. Again, this is something you can discuss and agree upon at the start of your circle. You will also discover what you need along the way.

There is no right or wrong way to do this. One challenge that may arise is someone speaking for a long time and no one feeling comfortable or sure about when, or whether, to stop or interrupt. This is something that happens in most, if not all, group process, so it is good to acknowledge it as a place of learning and exploration. As with most elements of collective process, there are times when it may be necessary for one woman to take more time. Conversely, some will also take less. What is critical is that there is a safe space in the circle to negotiate these details. What you want to avoid is anyone ever feeling guilt or blame for talking too much or too little.

It is also possible to be creative in approaching this checking-in time. We have at times begun with a writing prompt which turned into a verbal check-in. We have also found other fun and supportive ways of checking-in. For example: using three to five sentences to share what you want to say (they can be long with many attached clauses and phrases) or focusing on a specific topic or theme. It is important that the speaking not take precedence over the writing.

4. Ensure Confidentiality and Emotional Safety

Creating an atmosphere and environment within your circle that is safe, supportive and nurturing is of utmost importance. To do so, you can talk about what helps you to feel comfortable and safe in the circle. Confidentiality is a way that we ensure emotional safety. We make an agreement about what we will and will not share with others outside the circle.

This is why it is important to pay attention to the ongoing process of the circle and to strive for the open participation of each person. Making an agreement that what is shared within the circle stays within the circle can be part of this. Periodically, it may also be important to re-affirm one's personal commitment to the circle and to ensure the circle is meeting the needs of those within it. Within our circle, we have come to value how journalling together creates a sense of comfort and safety. It becomes a place for us to truly be ourselves.

5. Develop Trust

The development of trust among the members of the circle, as well as within each individual, helps determine the sustainability and depth possible. Confidentiality is a trust-building tool. It can feel very vulnerable to share your raw, immediate, personal writing with others. Without a trusting, safe environment, there can be no real open and honest communication and the atmosphere cannot support the sharing that is desired.

Trust is something that must be nurtured and allowed time to gestate and develop. Expecting everyone to immediately be open with one another is unrealistic and can lead to frustration and disappointment. It is better to recognize that each of us comes to the circle with our own experiences with trust. Each circle will evolve its own dynamic. It is important to allow the process to unfold. Remember, it is always a choice whether or not to share. Silence is a voice, too!

6. Share Food

Bringing and sharing food enhances the environment within the circle. While eating should not be the primary purpose of getting together, it can create feelings of nurturance and pleasure. Not all of us can consume the same kinds of food and some of us have dietary needs and restrictions. These should be discussed among the members of the circle. Also, not everyone has the time to prepare or the financial resources to support bringing complicated or expensive food to share. The importance is that each person feels comfortable with what she is bringing. Sharing food is something the circle creates together for the benefit of all of its members.

7. Write Together

Last but not least, create commonality by journalling together. What grounds us in this process is our coming together to write and share. We connect with one another within this sacred space of journalling together. This becomes our common ground and the foundation for our circle's cohesion. In this way, we create records for ourselves and can track the subjects, issues and themes that emerge from going to the page.

Imagine you are sitting in a circle of women and you are ready to start. You are probably feeling excited, nervous, curious. What will happen next? How will this work? We asked the same questions and felt the same feelings too. We dove in. We did what we knew how to do: we wrote and then the other steps followed.

Next, you will read about the four practices we discovered were necessary in cultivating Writing Alone Together.

Part Three:

Pen to Paper

Each time we pose
pen or pencil to paper
we connect with
who we are
who we were
who we want to be.

—Wendy

The Four Practices

Beginning is difficult. We are afraid of failing. We are afraid we will have nothing to say. We are afraid that what we will say will be banal or boring. We are afraid it may endanger us. We are afraid it may be a lie. We are afraid that what we say may be the truth. We are afraid of succeeding. We are afraid no one will notice. We are afraid someone will learn what we've said—and it may be ourselves.

—DEENA METZGER

It might feel like a quantum leap to take this typically very private act of journal writing and bring it into a circle. So often our beginnings as journal writers include keeping or even hiding our journals (among them diaries, notebooks, letters) in a private place for no one else to find or, more importantly, read. In fact, many people choose not to journal for fear that some-one will find and read their words—and that some-thing horrible will happen—perhaps they will be misunderstood, judged, someone might be hurt by what he or she reads, take the writing out of context or use it against the writer. The list of perceived fears or dire consequences attached to the perception of sharing private writing is common.

Through our journey together on the page, we recognized there are four essential practices in Writing Alone Together:

1. **Writing Freely**

2. **Reading Aloud**

3. **Listening Deeply**

4. **Bearing Witness**

These vital practices will support you to create a safe and intimate space for your circle to develop and expand your experience of journal writing within a circle of women.

1. Writing Freely

One of the greatest gifts that you can bring to your journal writing is your own inward permission to write freely.

—STEPHANIE DOWRICK

There are no shoulds or oughts, no one correct way. There is only your way. Whatever feels right for you is the right way to do the exercises. Elaborate on them or depart from them altogether. There are no rules here, only suggestions and ideas for you to try out. Explore and experiment.

—LUCIA CAPACCHIONE

Allowing ourselves to write freely is an essential feature of Writing Alone Together. The essence of writing freely is to follow one's own impulses and put down whatever comes. We start with a word, phrase, memory, image, question, quote, feeling or body sensation. There are hundreds of ways to come to the page. The point is to start writing and keep writing, returning to the page again and again.

Wendy Writes...

We begin with feelings. We begin with thoughts. We begin with words. There is no one way to begin, to start writing together. It is a process that begins when we come together and write. We offer each other prompts, exercises. We allow ourselves to open to whatever comes. We are creating our lives as we follow the impulse that comes from within. We become our own guides, support systems, mentors. And it is our job, our role—if we choose—to accept whatever comes without judgment, without criticism, without opposition.

There is a synergy when we are in a room writing together that brings us into more depth and resonance than when we are writing alone. Listening to the other writers' pens brushing against the paper is both exciting and calming. I am at once alone and connected.

Sometimes the writing takes us to very different places and directions. This is what is so dynamic and intriguing about writing together with others. There is no one correct way. Whatever you write is right! We each flow in our own direction. We try not to judge or compare ourselves to one another. To write freely, we must feel secure and safe in the process so we can guide our writing in whatever direction we (or it) may choose.

Recognizing Blocks and Resistance

Writing truthfully brings us face to face with our deepest resistances and also our greatest potential. Our ally on the journey is an openness that allows us to see what we've held apart from ourselves and invite it back into the whole. The writing that comes from this has a depth and texture, an authenticity. Censoring cuts off vitality, the life blood of our writing.

—LORRAINE GANE

Don't be afraid to tell the truth.

—FERRON

As we give ourselves permission to write freely, we are often faced with blocks or feelings of resistance that can get in the way of expressing ourselves fully. Negative self-talk, limiting beliefs, fears and doubts, as well as old habits and patterns, can constrict our overall sense of freedom, ease, confidence and well-being while writing.

Blocks and resistance can manifest in unique ways within each of us, for example, through procrastination, distraction, critical thoughts, censoring and "writer's block." These blocks or resistances can prevent us from journalling and might limit us in terms of what we will allow ourselves to consider writing about, which means that certain things fail to get expressed on the page. These unexpressed thoughts can also contribute to the negative judgments we have about ourselves and our writing, criticizing what we manage to get down on the page.

In order to become familiar with your own blocks and feelings of resistance, we invite you to consider these questions:

- What blocks or feelings of resistance are you aware of, or noticing, that might stop you from writing freely?

- What prevents you from fully expressing yourself in your journal?

We have learned it is important to notice and write about what gets in the way, to express those feelings that restrict our openness instead of forcing them down or pretending they do not exist. Writing about our blocks increases self-awareness and can also clear and release them, so they no longer limit our freedom or full potential on the page.

The act of giving voice to these blocks helps us to be in touch with other feelings within us. As we share our blocks and resistances, we move toward greater acceptance of ourselves and our writing. This creates a greater sense of freedom and trust in our writing practice and within our circle. To move through these blocks takes presence and awareness, both of which are also nurtured through writing.

Blocks or resistance can feel confusing, overwhelming and frustrating. However, when we allow ourselves to notice these feelings and blocks, we can reframe this resistance into self-acceptance and enter a more authentic relationship with ourselves and our writing.

—HANNAH BRAIME

Tips For Writing Freely:

- Take a few minutes to breathe deeply and connect with your body

- Keep your pen, pencil or fingers on the keypad moving

- Don't worry about spelling, punctuation or grammar

- Experiment, take risks, be bold, exaggerate

- Acknowledge differing or conflicting thoughts and feelings

- Identify and explore blocks and resistance

- Allow yourself to move from one subject to the next

- Ask questions to expand your ideas and perspectives

- Be curious and open to whatever comes

- Whatever you write is right

2. Reading Aloud

Reading aloud releases the tension, allows you to connect with what you actually write… It allows you to hear yourself, mirrored back from the silent mind of the listening.

—NATALIE GOLDBERG

I have come to believe over and over again that what is most important to me must be spoken, made verbal and shared, even at the risk of having it bruised or misunderstood.

—Audre Lorde

And yet I want to try it, this difficult task of voicing. Perhaps I need it, perhaps we all need it, this translation from the language of the source, this labour of love, where we all try to reach one another, each with our own strange words.

—Burghild Nina Holzer

Reading our writing aloud can be profound. A palpable change occurs as we read aloud our own words, our nascent, just-appearing thoughts. We become both the speaker and the listener, writer and reader. We hear ourselves and feel our words in a richer way. This creates intimacy, compassion and connection within the circle and deepens self-awareness all at once. We allow ourselves to be seen and to be vulnerable.

Ahava Writes...

There is something absolutely scrumptious about reading my poetry aloud. I use that word purposely. I love the way it feels to speak the words, savouring their sounds and shapes and meanings on my tongue, how they slip out of my mouth like the songs of birds. I guess that's a part of it, they are my singing. It is so natural for me to speak them.

If you have never felt comfortable speaking your words aloud, or even if you are adept at talking in front of large groups of people, it may feel strange to share your journal entries. We encourage you to try. Start by sharing a few sentences or phrases. Part of the difficulty is that we are not used to saying things so openly. They are your words so it's up to you to share them as it feels right for you.

Lynda Writes...

I have come to appreciate reading aloud as an integral part of my creative and journal writing practice. Reading aloud shapes my writing, hones my voice and gives sound to words, which allows the meaning of the words to resonate more deeply for me and hopefully for the listener, too. One of my favourite parts of our Writing Alone Together group has included having the opportunity to read my writing aloud and to hear Ahava's and Wendy's writing, too. It is nourishing, entertaining and informative to be read to, like how my sons must feel when I read to them. It is sometimes risky and scary, too, a sign of heart and vulnerability. It is a radical act to write for oneself and it is a transformational act to share that writing aloud with others.

Sharing our writing aloud with one another creates a safe place to share without judgment and criticism. As we consciously connect with ourselves, we cultivate authentic connections and trust with one another. This breathes life into our writing and courage into our souls. When we read aloud, we connect with the feelings and emotions of our words, which may not be apparent when we are writing them down or reading them silently to ourselves. It is natural to feel vulnerable, hesitant, frightened and uncertain when reading our words aloud. We may also feel excited, enthusiastic and eager.

Wendy Writes...

At some point during my writing workshops, when someone is reading aloud what she's written, her voice will begin to crack and suddenly tears begin to flow. Often a person apologizes for this emotional display. I reassure her there is nothing wrong with tears or revealing our emotional reactions to what we're reading. Personally, this reinforces my belief in the healing aspects of reading our writing aloud.

Sometimes, reading your writing aloud is not the best thing to do. For example, if you have written about something traumatic, there is the risk of being retraumatized by reading it aloud. It is up to each woman to decide this for herself. This is why reading aloud is always a choice. If you start to read and feel distressed, allow yourself to stop. The same is true for writing itself. If you ever feel like you are being wounded from the writing, stop, take a break, care for yourself.

> *Owning our story can be hard but not nearly as difficult as spending our lives running from it. Embracing our vulnerabilities is risky but not nearly as dangerous as giving up on love and belonging and joy—the experiences that make us the most vulnerable.*
>
> —BRENE BROWN

Tips For Reading Aloud:

- Sharing is always voluntary

- Take a few deep breaths before speaking your words aloud

- Speak slowly and loud enough to be heard

- You can choose to read a word, line, phrase, paragraph or the whole entry

- It is natural for emotions to arise when reading

- Stay connected to your breath as you read

- If you choose not to share your writing, share how it felt to write, what you wrote about or what the topic meant to you

3. Listening Deeply

Listening means hearing without judging...the practice of listening also means listening without an agenda. If you are thinking ahead, you are likely not listening. If you are planning what you want to say, you are not really listening.

—MAUREEN FITZGERALD

If I surrender
to what you're saying,
if I take a listening role
while you're talking,
I take in what you are saying, I receive.

—MARION WOODMAN

How we listen to one another is important when sharing our journal writing. Listening means being receptive to what is being shared and also hearing beyond the words. When one woman is reading her writing aloud, the others are there to listen with utmost, open attention. This is essential towards building trust in the circle. Listening also implies being non-judgmental.

By paying attention to our own responses as we listen, we guard against letting them affect the reader. We each carry within us beliefs, prejudices and preferences. We may sometimes unknowingly reveal these prejudices without speaking, through our body language or facial expression. This inner/outer listening is helpful in keeping the circle safe and open. Caring and empathy arise naturally as we get to know circle members through our writing. We do not need to heal or fix one another. What a relief it is to not "have to do" anything about what we are hearing. We listen, allow and let it be.

As we listen to another's writing, difficult feelings may arise. It is our responsibility as listeners to notice the feelings that are arising in the moment and then to return to listening to the reader's voice and words. Writing Alone Together is about learning how to be with others in ways that respect differences. We let the process teach us to cultivate curiosity in place of prejudice, honour ambiguity over animosity and to value possibility over limited perception. This is how the practices are transformational. We bring the whole of ourselves and are accepted for all of who we are.

Ahava Writes...

Let's learn to make a difference by listening to each other... how else are we going to hear what's going to save us if we don't listen and create a space? This is not about consuming but expressing, not about becoming someone else, looking better and cooler and hotter but being all of who we are, here, now, together.

This process is different from most other writing circle practices in that we don't engage in critique— we don't offer our writing up for scrutiny or judgment. The writing just is. This element allows us to feel open without the fear of receiving criticism from others.

Ahava Writes...

Anxiety. Are you going to critique my writing? My writing is not for critique. It's for revelation, making my unknown known, exercising my spirituality, celebrating the moments of my life, like climbing the ladder to the top of the cherry tree and feeling the fear of being so high up, recognizing this is the first time and no wonder I feel afraid but I will learn to climb this ladder, to pick the cherries and plums and apples and pears. It'll just take time, practice, attention, compassion.

Our goal is not to suppress our reactions to what is being said, but to limit "critical" responses. After a writer has read, we share our feelings, impressions and, most importantly, our supportive comments.

Here are some phrases you may wish to use in offering appreciation:

- What I appreciate about what you wrote is…

- What resonates with me is…

- What most stands out for me is…

- What surprises me is…

- What I am now curious about is…

- What was moving for me is…

- What was powerful for me is…

By offering this positive, validating feedback, each writer can stay open without the added vulnerability of receiving criticism from others.

A format that prioritizes sharing without critique enables us to suspend judgment and internal doubts and to be authentic with our writing, our thoughts, our words and one another. This is a journal writing circle, not a writing critique group. We have found this kind of approach through presence and listening allows us to be companions and sister writers.

Lynda Writes...

Imagine our relationships, workplaces, politics and world with a greater capacity for listening deeply. Imagine more peace, less conflict and greater health for individuals and the whole. Listening teaches how to hear what needs and wants to be heard. Being heard helps us love ourselves and each other and even those we haven't met yet.

Tips For Listening Deeply:

- Stay open to what is being said
- Listen with all of your senses (whole body listening)
- Notice and suspend your judgments, prejudices and assumptions
- Do not interrupt someone who is speaking
- Share supportive affirmations
- Honour the words being spoken
- Listen to connect, empathize and understand

4. Bearing Witness

When I bear witness I turn toward another and am willing to let their experience enter my heart. I step into the picture, by being willing to be open to their experience, to not turn away my gaze.... We can feel hopeless and

*overwhelmed by this world; we can turn away and just
live the best life we can. Or we can learn to bear witness.*

—Margaret Wheatley

*The ability to reflect on one's experience is a key capacity
that fosters resilience. It allows one to witness the self and
to witness others… The capacity to witness the self is
linked to having an appreciative listener, someone with
whom one can share honestly.*

—Kathie Weingarten

When we write and share our journal writing with one
another, we are agreeing to be vulnerable, to be seen
with aspects of ourselves that are often very quiet, private parts of our inner worlds. As we share our writing,
we are saying, "I am prepared to be seen by you, to be
witnessed. I trust that you will hold this with respect
and care." We move into our hearts as we share this
intimate experience in our circle.

Bearing witness asks us to be fully present and hold
the space for one another. It is a way of interacting
with respect for another human being that honours
who they are and what they are sharing. It is a skill and
a decision to show up for one another with commitment and engagement. This enables us to truly see one
another in authentic, honest ways—so we may also see
ourselves with this level of kindness and depth. This
involves paying attention to life as it is happening, being supportive and offering affirmation.

Lynda Writes...

*I love hearing what you liked, what most stood out for each of you
when you heard my words, learning how my writing lands when
it is given voice. I love the warm feeling of appreciation that*

washes over me in the presence of being seen, heard and champi-oned. And yes, when the writing dips me into the tingling of my stirred heart, and tears might fall, or laughter dances across the page, or anger bubbles—that you can both hold the space for the heart of my writing and my process—without having to fix or cajole—but simply be with me in courageous, bold, wide open places so I can fly on the wings of my writing and be where it wants to take me fully. I trust you to know that I am strong and brave and that I want to feel my writing, feel my life.

You will see from our journal writing in Part Five—written together and then shared with one another and now with you—we are writing from some of our most vulnerable, honest and raw places. Choosing to be and share with one another in this way is a sacred and bold act. Bearing witness creates the safe, respectful and trusting emotional space for this type of sharing. Through this witnessing, we can reach deeper levels of empathy and compassion for one another, which leads to greater presence, sharing, learning and growth.

Tips For Bearing Witness:

- Validate one another's openness and honesty
- Appreciate one another for sharing
- Allow the reader to experience their full emotional expression
- Honour the heart of the story and the storyteller
- Acknowledge the humanity or "beingness" of one another

Part Four:

Moment by Moment

My writing life is being claimed
moment by moment.
I am naming it as such,
saying out loud
"I am a writer."

—**Lynda**

The Seven Principles

Through our journey of Writing Alone Together, recurring themes and benefits kept surfacing within our individual writing and in our shared conversations. We refer to these as the Seven Principles. They are qualities that are nurtured as you work with the Four Practices. They are both extensions of the practices and gifts that come through Writing Alone Together.

We invite you to explore them to discover their meaning and value within your own circle of journal writing.

1. Grounding in the Moment

2. Slowing Down and Paying Attention

3. Developing Intimacy

4. Trusting Your Own Experience

5. Unleashing Creativity

6. Acknowledging Conflicts and Differences

7. Exploring the Personal as Political

1. Grounding in the Moment

The first step is this: Stop. By this I mean, Sit still for a moment. It doesn't need to be a long moment; a few deep breaths, enough to clear your head and center yourself in your body. The point is simply to experience your own awareness, without your thoughts chasing after the past or future.

—KIM ADDONIZIO

There is only this moment, this night, this remembrance rolling towards you from the distant past, this blank page, this inspiration yielding itself to you.

—ARIEL GORE

How does journal writing ground us in the moment? When we come to the page, we bring our whole selves: our current worries and fears, joys and gratitude, physical aches and emotional challenges. And we come here. Where is here? Here is this very instant when your hand marks the page with your pen or pencil or taps the keys on the keyboard. Here is also what is happening to you, inside you and around you, at the very moment of writing. Here is an unfolding storyline that is ever-changing, becoming transformed when you mark the page with your momentary words.

Ahava Writes...

We use our senses to ground in the moment, to become present. When we take up our pen and our fingers begin the waltz, tips of flesh on black letters on white dance floor, we are here. We hear the breath as it moves in and out of our noses or mouths. We feel the soft lap of the couch or window seat or desk chair against our butt and thighs. We feel the air in the room on our cheeks, the backs of our hands and whatever is rubbing against our arms or legs, whether it's the fabric of our clothes, the dog or the edge of the blanket. We see the birds out the window or the rain through the skylight or the steam rising from the kettle.

Being fully here with our ears, eyes, nose, mouth, awake to our physical experience, is how we ground. We use the light, the temperature, the hard surfaces under our feet, the action of our hands to alert us to the fact we are here. We know then that we are in this moment.

As we begin writing, we start from this present moment and our mind moves in many directions. And we let it. We watch our mind and write out its contents. And after a while—maybe five or ten minutes, or longer if we are in the flow of the writing—we pause and listen again to the breath, the fridge, the birds, our heartbeats. We keep coming back to this sensual, physical experience—this seeing, hearing, feeling, tasting and smelling of our present-moment awareness as our grounding. We start from here. Every time.

Tips For Grounding in the Moment:

- Become aware of your physical body: feel the sensations where your clothes meet your skin, your thighs meet the chair or the pressure where your hands meet the page or the keys

- Notice how your breath is circulating through your body: feel the coolness of your breath as it enters or leaves your nostrils or the expansion as it fills your chest or belly

- Listen to the sounds inside and around you: hear the pulse of your heartbeat, the grumble of your belly, the chirps of birds or the hum of silence

2. Slowing Down and Paying Attention

More and more people are tired of the fast paced frenzied 'information-age' and are interested in higher-quality lives—lives in which they have more time for themselves and their relationships, more energy to invest in their emotional, physical, and spiritual well-being.

—CHERYL RICHARDSON

Our job is to wake up to everything, because if we slow down enough, we see that we are everything.

—NATALIE GOLDBERG

Slowing down and paying attention is an art form. In our often busy lives as women, it is easy to become disconnected from our center, from ourselves and from others. This can lead to higher levels of stress and discontent. Our lives can feel like a whirlwind, speeding up as we try to take on more and more tasks and functions, leaving us little time to focus on our own self-care and creative needs.

Writing Alone Together helps us create a relaxing and contemplative space in which we can reconnect with ourselves. As we witness other women slowing down, we gain support and encouragement to do it ourselves.

Lynda Writes...

As the mother of two young sons, a wife, an entrepreneur with two businesses, a writer, a daughter to aging parents, and a woman who believes in practicing self-care as foundational to my own health, wellness, balance and happiness—I understand busy! I understand the often elusive, fleeting nature of balance. Most days I feel like I am juggling alligators—up at 6 a.m., get breakfast on the table, snacks, lunches, pack the boys' backpacks, check my schedule for the day, get myself and our children out the door, work as a team with my honey to keep all the balls in the air, drive our neighbour to the head of the harbour so he can hitchhike to town, serve my coaching clients, write articles, update my blog, facilitate writing retreats, set off for a walk trying to ensure daily exercise or at least some semblance of movement beyond bending over to wipe up the next spill, eat an apple, return phone calls, market our business, promote my next coaching group, pick up the kids, help prepare dinner, run the baths, get the pajamas out, read stories, call my mother, check email, load the dishwasher, connect with my husband, pay bills, write a thank you note to put in the mail tomorrow, fold laundry, find matching socks, put the boys' clothes out for the next day, write in my journal, breathe, stretch, turn out the lights...perhaps you can relate? As a multi-tasking high achiever, I always appreciate the efficiency and also wide open freedom that my journal writing practice offers me.

The journal is a place to slow down, notice and pay attention. It allows us to be an observer and to be fully engaged with life at the same time. We can recognize patterns, passions and mistakes on the page. We can make decisions, brainstorm options, vent frustrations and dream possibilities as the pen moves across the paper. The very act of stopping, sitting down, picking up the journal and pen and starting to write is a form of self-care. We show ourselves our life matters, that our thoughts, feelings, ideas and experiences are worthy of noting. We are worthy of this time to reflect and replenish.

Slowing down and paying attention are not frivolous acts; they are essential to health, wellness and quality of life. Without an inner sense of peace and calm, it is very easy to be tossed away, to get lost in the fast pace of modern life. When we slow down, we engage the parasympathetic nervous system, which triggers our bodies' relaxation response. Our blood pressure lowers, our breath deepens and our minds become quieter, with less mental chatter, which allows us to focus on the present moment. Our writing can flow more easily from a relaxed, present mind. As our bodies settle and our pulse slows, we also become more open to inspiration and to feeling our interconnection with all life.

Tips For Slowing Down and Paying Attention:

- Before beginning to write together, take a few moments to breathe and connect with yourself

- After writing in your journal or reading your words, do not judge or criticize what you've written. Accept it as an expression of where you are at this moment

- When you notice your mind wandering, stop and focus on what's happening in your body in the present moment

3. Developing Intimacy

By sharing my intimate world, I inspire others to do the same, to move beyond shame and protection and to say what we see, what we have lived, to affirm that in its full worth.

—ELLEN BASS

Intimacy with the self takes time to develop. We must earn our own trust by listening attentively and without judgment, by giving ourselves quality time, by attending to our own needs and desires with generosity and patience, and by honoring our ever-shifting emotions.

—KAY LEIGH HAGEN

The relationship with the self is central to self-care; jour-
nal writing is a means of developing intimacy with and
knowledge of the self.

—KATE THOMPSON

There are different kinds of intimacy developed through Writing Alone Together: intimacy with the self, intimacy with the circle, intimacy with our writing and intimacy with the world.

Self-intimacy does not come immediately. It is a process that develops each time we have the courage to be honest with ourselves, to acknowledge our thoughts and feelings and accept them as we write them down on the page. One way to think of intimacy is *in-to-me-see*. Through knowing our own desires, insecurities, questions, challenges and successes, we discover who we are and how we relate to the world. The more we write, the more we get to know who we are, how we feel and what we care about.

This intimacy with ourselves grows as we recognize the patterns and subjects we keep writing about. How we put words together and our particular writing styles also become apparent the more we write and share our words with others.

None of us writes in a vacuum. We are all a part of this maddeningly beautiful world and our words are full of that beautiful madness. When we write we participate in the beauty and we acknowledge the pain, anger, frustration, joy and other emotions. Writing is life—it reflects all the myriad tones and textures of our experiences back to us. We write to sustain ourselves, to keep ourselves balanced and sane. We write to connect, to tell the truth as much as we know it in the moment and as we change.

Connecting to these changes with awareness is at the heart of self-intimacy—the growing knowing of the self.

Wendy Writes...

I crave intimacy—sharing with others in depth and with abandon is what I live for. It is a deep craving and, at times, a source of pain and disappointment. For when the intimacy I desire doesn't manifest or ceases to exist, I mourn its loss and wallow in upset. The beauty of journal writing—of writing for oneself—is that you are always within reach, never totally abandoned as you literally show up for yourself and follow your own lead. I write despair and loss and pain. I write joy and ecstasy and freedom. I can go into the heart of the matter, the feeling at hand, or soar away into complete fantasy and abstraction. My writing can pierce the skin and find trickles and pools of blood. It can open up wide vistas of vision and possibility, integrating all aspects of myself, owning it all, acknowledging complexities and contradictions. I write intimacy by writing it all. As the pages are filled, as the years are lived, I continue to be present in this life.

Tips For Developing Intimacy:

- Go to the page with all of who you are: your joys and hurts, loves and losses, successes and failures

- Write about the parts of you that you like as well as the parts of you that are more challenging to accept

- Listen with your heart to what each woman has to share and be open to the connections between her words and yours

4. Trusting Your Own Experience

*I get to tell my truth. I get to seek meaning and realiza-
tion. I get to live fully, wildly, imperfectly. That's why
I'm alive. And all I actually have to offer as a writer is
my version of life. Every single thing that has happened
to me is mine.*

—ANNE LAMOTT

*The personal life deeply lived always expands into truths
beyond itself.*

—ANAÏS NIN

*Once we are in the flow
of our life's river,
we experience synchronicity.
Outer and inner
become
much the same.*

—MARION WOODMAN

When we connect with and acknowledge our authentic feelings, we are more apt to trust our own experiences and instincts. This feeling of trust empowers
us to listen within for our own answers and access a
deeper sense of meaning in our lives.

Journalling requires we trust the process of writing
itself because we can never truly predict where our
writing will take us in any given moment. In this surrender, we practice the ability to trust ourselves, our
voice and our stories. This builds confidence and compassion in our ability for self-expression both within
our journals and in our lives.

Wendy Writes...

This power of writing the truth of our lives resonates whether the form of personal writing is autobiography, memoir, narrative, diary, journal or life story. Writing from our lived experience reveals our feelings, emotions and perspectives, which are constantly transforming as we move through our lives.

I was compelled to share with others the letter I wrote to my parents about coming out as a lesbian. It was an act of liberation. Not just the writing of the letter—naming myself, showing my vulnerability—but in sending it and in the horrendous response I received from them. But then, as writing has always been a means of not only self-reflection and discovery but also affirmation, support and healing, I brought it into the light for others to read and to experience for their own validation or caution.

Journalling is an empowered way of understanding our lives from a place of curiosity. We can wonder about what we think, feel, believe, want and need. Journalling helps us turn inward to ask powerful questions and to listen for the answers and access guidance that is always within. We live in times in which there are so many gurus, teachers, helpers, healers and people who are devoted to drawing out the essential goodness and inherent well-being in us all. We have been conditioned to turn to experts for advice, direction and guidance. This can disconnect us from our inner knowing. Instead of turning somewhere outside of ourselves for direction, we can pick up our pens and write into the heart and wisdom of our own being.

Journal writing encourages us to prioritize our own personal sense of our lives and allows us to increase our trust in our own perspectives and ideas. We also gain an ability to reflect upon our experiences as we look back in time and re-construct our feelings about those experiences. As well, we practice the ability to trust our intuition and impulses, as we can never predict where our writing will or can take us.

When we honour this relationship we have with ourselves and with our lives, we grow in our ability to trust our own experiences and answer our own questions.

Lynda Writes...

We all have times in our lives in which we get lost, lose our way, get confused, aren't sure what to do next, times when we are making difficult decisions and when we crave greater clarity. When I was in my late twenties, I was married and my husband and I were going through some very difficult times. Eventually these challenges led to us living apart and entering an era of being "separated." During this time, we went for counselling, continued to go for coffee dates at Tim Horton's, saw the odd Tuesday night movie together, and were otherwise pleasant with each other. Our hearts were also breaking. We were lost, unsure how or if to move forward in our marriage together.

I talked to lots of friends, my family, the counsellor, colleagues and anyone who might listen about my confusion and situation. While talking out loud offered certain release and reassurance, the most comforting and reliable and soulful place for me to show up during this emotionally overwhelming and painful time, was in the pages of my journal. For showing up there was the same as coming home and showing up within myself, something that in some ways, I had stopped doing in our marriage. I was surrendering my needs, desires, dreams and truth within the reality of our struggling marriage, stuffing my longings, my instincts, and my knowing into organized sock drawers, a tidy walk-in closet, and confining spaces in my heart and soul.

But in my journal, I was free to be me. I was free to be afraid, unsure, whole, broken, confused, all right, not all right, strong, weak, grief stricken…on the blank page I felt held, known, loved. Through writing for myself over and over again, I saw the truth of my decision. First I wrote the truth, that I wanted to get a divorce, and then once I trusted this truth, trusted myself and my own decision making, I spoke this truth out loud. That was in 1999. We had our last counselling session, our last cup of coffee, saw our last movie together. Our separation was over and our divorce process began. I cried myself to sleep for months. I trusted my own experience, even though it was a painful time. I knew I could do this, first and foremost, because my regular journal writing taught me the power of trusting the words and feelings that tumbled from my heart to the page. My truth revealed itself to me. All I had to do was trust it and move forward. And I did.

… At last I understood that writing was this: an impulse to share with other people a feeling or truth I had myself.

—Brenda Ueland

Tips For Trusting Your Own Experience:

- Ask yourself a powerful question and then respond to it in your writing

- Give yourself permission to reveal your authentic feelings on the page

- Surrender to the unique, intuitive flow of your writing

5. Unleashing Creativity

Through the play of our imagination, we gain the power to expand our limits, to integrate change and to guide our personal growth. Writing releases us into a timeless world where all things are possible.

—Kimberley Snow

Learning to trust the possible and to accept what arises, to welcome surprise and the ways of the Trickster, not to censor too quickly—all lessons necessary for a writer.

—JANE HIRSHFIELD

Putting our fingers on the keyboard or our pens on the page unleashes our creativity. We don't know what's going to emerge when we take the leap. Journalling gives us confidence to play, to enter a space of not-knowing and discover new wor(l)ds as we go.

At times we have to step back and look at what we do because it can become so habitual we don't notice that we're doing it. As in any activity we partake in over and over again, we can get stale and become overly accustomed to saying the same old things. When we keep things interesting and fresh, we are able to surprise ourselves, learn something new about who we are and the world we live in.

Ahava Writes...

One of the most exciting things for me about journal writing is how it has enabled me to develop my creative skills as a poet, playwright, improvisational storyteller and performer. My practice of journal writing has allowed me to explore these different language art forms and to trust and follow the words as they land, no matter what they initially sound or look like. It takes courage and a willingness to be surprised, amazed and confused by what you write. It takes a willingness to not know what you are writing about even as the words keep on flowing.

If I hadn't learned through my practice of journal writing that it was okay to be "the fool," to let the words take me where my imagination and intuition wanted them to go, then I never would have written a play about a woman who works at a strip club and has a regular customer who only shows up once a month

65

dressed in red and invites her to dance differently, nor completed a PhD thesis using the gates of the farm where I live as metaphors for the process of opening the heart into relationship. I also never would have published a whole book of poems about healing from sexual abuse and eating disorders, nor a poetry CD about my relationship to nature and lovers.

Journal writing teaches us about the nature of creativity. It helps us become more awake, expansive and open in all areas of our life. It offers a way to foster a sense of wonder. Often as journal writers we are surprised by ideas, feelings and topics that are revealed to us as a direct result of the writing process itself. When we surrender our need to know and release our need for control, new awareness can emerge or blossom. The parts of ourselves that we might tend to resist can only be embraced once we see them and the only way to make these aspects of the self visible is to be willing to go into the unknown.

Creativity draws us into the mystery of our lives, into the unknown. Many people are afraid of the unknown, especially the unknown parts of themselves that open through self-reflection and practices that call them into greater self-awareness. Journalling, in particular, requires that we surrender and have faith in where the writing might take us, which is often into the unknown. This reveals one of the challenges of embracing our creativity.

If we practice it, if we enter the inner world, we find ourselves outside the perimeter of conventional society—outsiders feeling all the loneliness of that disconnection. And yet we are simultaneously as far as we can get from loneliness because we are, finally, with ourselves.

—DEENA METZGER

Writing Alone Together fosters an alchemy of ideas. We are exposed not only to our own unknown, our own surprising emergence, but also to that of others. In witnessing this diversity of voice, experience and expression, we are invited further into our own. We are taught what is possible by being exposed to others' creative expression. We allow our writing to inspire us into conversation and contemplation about themes in our lives. We create new meanings. We create new selves. Creativity becomes a way of being, not just something we do.

Tips For Unleashing Creativity:

*   Have faith in where the writing might take you

*   Be willing to be surprised, amazed and confused by what you write

*   Honour the spontaneous emergence of new voices, stories and poems

6. Acknowledging Conflicts and Differences

I urge each one of us here to reach down into that deep place of knowledge inside herself and touch that terror and loathing of any difference that lives there. See whose face it wears.

—AUDRE LORDE

I write to learn how I live and how I want to live, to understand who I am and who I am becoming. I write to understand myself and my relationships with others. And yet when I write I discover what I do not know as well as what I know.

—CYNTHIA CHAMBERS

One of the most beneficial aspects of Writing Alone Together is learning to accept and honour differences. This doesn't necessarily come naturally, as many of us have been raised and socialized to be afraid of or distrust difference. In some cases we may even have been taught to hate those different from ourselves, or to ignore the parts of us that don't conform, whether with our families, friends or popular culture.

Ahava Writes...

In my journal and in the poems that emerged through the practice of free writing, I found the space to talk about the ways my family used to speak of other people in our lives who were different than us. When I started to write, I became aware of how ashamed and confused I was by the derogatory language they used when referring to blacks as "shvartzes" or non-Jews as "goyim." These Yiddish words were not harmless. They painted a picture for me of a world where white people were special and more important than people of other colours, faiths, languages. In a poem I wrote called "Ugly Once," I explored the divide between the culture I was raised in and those I grew up disdaining. The words, and the emotions I was attempting to express through them, became a bridge toward healing.

Through meeting, sharing and connecting in a circle, we develop a more expansive way of viewing both ourselves and others. Hearing others struggle with similar issues to our own can be comforting, and help bring them into perspective. We take the time to listen and find out how others feel and experience their lives.

Recognizing our often conflicted or ambivalent feelings encourages us to embrace the complexity of our lives. Conflicts and differences arise naturally in relationships, circles and other social interactions.

They may stem from differences in ages, social and economic classes, ethnicities, cultures, nationalities, gender identities, sexual orientations, personal preferences or practices, or because of divergent views, core beliefs, values, ideas, perspectives, politics or personalities. Whatever these differences are, they can become sources of increased understanding, prompting us to constructively recognize our assumptions about one another. They can also trigger other more destructive responses including alienation, judgment or stereotyping, which can then lead to escalated tension and emotional upset.

Wendy Writes...

I was able to express some of my insecurities—about my life, my work, even my writing—within our journal writing sessions together. This intimate level of sharing supported me in becoming more accepting of the place I was at and aware of the physical changes and issues I was experiencing with aging and fears of illness which permeate my thoughts but don't always have outlets for expression. Journal writing—and the deep level of sharing— was key to being allowed and encouraged to explore some of these difficult areas.

Acknowledging the conflicts and differences that arise in the circle can lead to increased awareness and compassion. It is helpful to take the time to process any conflicts that might have occurred and to address the feelings and concerns with the intention of bringing empathy and understanding to the circle. We may also decide to put it aside for a later time.

While this is not always easy, conflict is always better handled when it is open rather than concealed, denied or ignored. It is good to remember conflict is not a reflection of a circle's failure. More likely, as in other close relationships, it is a measure of a circle's increased intimacy.

At the core of conflict is an invitation for learning and growth. When differences are handled with an open mind and caring heart, no one is made to be wrong and everyone is respected and heard. Within any conflict is an opportunity for increased closeness and renewed commitment to the circle.

Tips For Acknowledging Conflicts and Differences:

- Check-in with each other when feelings of discomfort or hurt surface

- If there is a conflict between two women in the circle, choose another woman as mediator to help create a safe space for listening and speaking

- Accept that you may not agree with everything everyone shares, but you can commit to being non-judgmental

7. Exploring the Personal as Political

Journal keeping becomes a powerful tool for personal and political change, providing an opportunity for women to develop the skill of self-observation, to practice self-love, and to document accurately the truth of our lives.

—Kay Leigh Hagan

Eat rice have faith in women
what I don't know now
I can still learn
slowly slowly

if I learn I can teach others
if others learn first
I must believe
they will serve back and teach me

—FRAN WINANT

When we as women come together to write and share stories, we are prompted to act ethically and bravely, challenge violence and oppression, acknowledge paradox and complexity and to live authentic, empowered lives. We view this very personal yet always political practice as activism. The early women's liberation and feminist movements introduced the concept of the intimate connection between the personal and political. This allows us to see that our personal experiences, issues and problems are also political issues and, reciprocally, that political realities, institutions and beliefs impact our individual lives. Every woman has her own unique life stories and narratives based on personal experiences and connected to social, cultural and political contexts.

Lynda Writes...

I was born in 1969. My birth mother was eighteen years old, pregnant, unmarried and Catholic. Her options, and my fate in such a "predicament," were largely determined for her by the social, cultural, religious and political realities of the times whereby she, and approximately 17,000 other women in Ontario alone that same year, had to give their babies up for adoption. My birth mother did not perceive herself as having any other choices; keeping me was not an option. She told me that when she was at the home for unwed mothers, the young women were encouraged "to forget that their babies had ever been born" and to believe "they are better off this way."

Feminism (or feminisms) is a foundational principle all three of us share. Because of our range in ages and experience, we have each been introduced to feminism at different times and in different ways. We greatly respect the powerful ways in which the women's movement has shaped our lives, our work, our roles, our visions and our beliefs about what is possible for us as women living in the twenty-first century.

Wendy Writes...

Feminism attracted me—inspired, fed, enriched and absolutely transformed my life—as a nineteen-year-old girl turning woman. The most influential tenet of this whole liberation movement was "the personal is political." This changed everything. No longer were my personal problems and constraints only my own, but they were also political, public issues. I was encouraged to see this relationship in every part of my life.

At twenty, when in college in Berkeley in the 1970s, I joined an anti-rape collective. I took classes with feminist teachers, feminist content and feminist perspectives. I devoured novels, essays, anthologies, stories, newspapers, newsletters, position papers by women. I saw the interconnections between sexism, racism, classism, capitalism, imperialism, ableism and heterosexism. I met with other women in living rooms, kitchens, classrooms, coffeehouses, conferences, offices, music festivals, bars, bookstores and beds! I sat down and listened and spoke (meekly at first) and read and wrote and discussed and theorized and collaborated and (sometimes) argued and disagreed with, but mostly felt in awe of the beauty, power, presence, rage, sensibility of these women among whom I was living and creating and becoming.

As a feminist, I bring this awareness into my life, my writing, my teaching, my work. This underscores the connections I feel with others. And writing is a constant companion, accompanying me on this journey towards myself, new worlds and ways of being.

I am forever indebted to this movement of women, these feminists throughout my life, throughout the world, risking all to bring our private lives into the light.

As women, we realized that our sense of connection grew because of our common perspective. We all acknowledge that feminism has inspired, nourished and guided us. Feminism is alive and present in our work. At its core, feminism is a living, evolving ideology about the complete equality of all.

Ahava Writes...

When I first began to write about the incest, my words focused on describing the particular environment in which it happened and how I must have felt as a young girl living in a chaotic two-family house with adults who didn't know how to take responsibility for their unhealthy behaviours but rather blamed, shamed and projected them onto others.

As I became exposed to feminism through work, colleagues, roommates and friends, I began to understand the roots of the abuse. Incest and other forms of violence against women are systemic not only to the Jewish culture but to all patriarchal religious and cultural traditions. As a Jewish girl educated in private Hebrew school, I had been raised on stories of girls and women whose lives had taken a back seat to the men, or worse—stories of women who were raped, abandoned, turned to stone—whose accomplishments had been ignored and undervalued. My mother told me about her own frustration when her father chose to NOT support her business education but went on to fund her younger brother. As a young woman growing up in the "video killed the radio star" `80s, media messages showed me that women were inferior, portrayed in magazines in sexualized, infantilized and disembodied positions. It was against these events and beliefs about women that I rallied my words.

73

In the journal I ranted over the injustices, raged against my own succumbing to the power play of my older cousin and fostered compassion for the girl I was at that time in that place, when there were so many other challenges I was facing all at once. In the journal with each line and every new poem I wrote, I began to craft a new vision for being a woman, drawing on inspiration from Jewish, feminist, lesbian writers and eco-philosophers including Mary Daly (Gyn/ecology), Susan Griffin (Woman and Nature: The Roaring Inside Her), Judith Plaskow (Standing Again at Sinai) and Marge Piercy (He, She and It)—each of whom offered me hope and encouragement through their daring and powerful alternative narratives.

We have been profoundly inspired by the wisdom of feminist writers, teachers and mentors who have forged their own paths, spoken out, taken stands, confronted inequities and resisted sexist rules. We celebrate women who have flaunted their truths, sustained their desires, loved and nurtured and kept at it, so others like ourselves could live in a more just, humane and caring world. And there is still much work to do for the new waves of feminism emerging in these times.

Tips For Exploring the Personal as Political:

- Write about the challenges you have faced as a girl or woman at home, school, work or in your community

- Connect your life stories to social, cultural and political contexts

- Celebrate the women whose voices and activism have made a difference in your life

Part Five:

Free Fall Words

I need my right hand to write.
To free fall words, ideas, feelings,
onto blank white paper.

—Lynda

Introduction to Our Journal Entries and Writing Prompts

You are writing to expand your perspectives, to create openings in your life, to advance the action in your personal story, to glimpse a different picture of yourself.

—LAURA CERWINSKE

Journalling is a form of free writing. We start at a certain place, often flowing from a prompt or theme, and we go where we go. We let the writing take us where it wants. Sometimes our journalling might not make any sense; sometimes it flows and sometimes it doesn't. The writing is random and part of a unified whole, called our lives. This is the nature of journalling—it is deep writing—taking us into the marrow of our stories, the meandering of our minds, the essence of feelings.

The following journal entries—written during the last seven years—are mostly unedited. When writing for ourselves we do not worry about grammar and punctuation and making total sense, we just write it all down. We invite you to read our journal entries with this in mind, knowing they are not meant to be perfect. They are spontaneous, the laying down of words to create self-awareness and awakening.

We ask you to read our writing with the Writing Alone Together practices in mind—to listen deeply and bear witness—for we have already written freely and read aloud. In receiving our journalling in this way, you bring your full presence and non-judgmental self to the foreground; this is a gift you give to us and to yourself. While you are reading our entries, you might think to yourself, "What is she talking about here?" or "That doesn't make any sense." Notice, take it all in and then let it inspire you.

Our journalling flows from the following themes which we offer to you as prompts and questions to go to the page.

1. **Writing Time Together**

2. **Right Now/Write Now**

3. **Embodiment**

4. **I Am Called**

5. **Quotations**

6. **Passion Statement**

7. **The Road Not Taken**

8. **Words We Do Not Have**

9. **Poetry**

10. **Dialogue Writing**

11. **Past, Present and Future**

12. **Writing Goals**

13. **Our Writing Life**

14. **Relating To The Term Writer**

15. **Rereading Our Journals**

1. Writing Time Together

You simply keep putting down one damn word after the other, as you hear them, as they come to you.

—ANNE LAMOTT

My experience is that writing in a group sparks a creative force that, if the writer trusts it and goes with it—can take the writing and the writer to unexpected, surprising places of memory and imagination.

—JUDY REEVES

For those of us who write, we understand that it takes time, sometimes the time we don't have because our lives are full of responsibilities and other activities. By defining a time to get together to write, we support one another to stay committed to what we love and know is good for us. A journal writing circle celebrates our successes and helps us cope with our setbacks. It also helps us be accountable and stay committed to our journalling. We know we are not alone. The sound of pens scratching paper in unison is an intimately beautiful song that praises the life we have been given and assures we stay open to each moment's varied melodies.

Journal Writing Prompt **Ask yourself: "What do I most want from our time together? How might this time be structured so it is of the most benefit?" Use this as an opportunity to explore the terrain of your thoughts and possibilities for journal writing with others.**

AHAVA

What I most want and need from this writing circle is a place to grapple with my desires to be out in the world as a writer and my fear of rejection and failure. I write and write and write and nothing is good enough. I don't want to send it out because it's not exactly where I'm at now and I'm afraid people are going to challenge me on my beliefs, tell me I'm wrong, judge my words, thoughts, being.

Yet I love sharing my writing aloud. I love speaking my words. I'm afraid to hurt someone, to be politically incorrect, so I don't. I'm afraid I will insult someone. I need a place to speak these fears, to honour them, understand them and challenge them. They are so big, visceral. I need to celebrate myself as a writer, not deny it. The tears all week at the poetry workshop were about that self-acceptance.

Why do I not let myself be? Why do I hoard my writing and not send it out?

I feel so much compassion for myself and so confused too. Because the act of writing is so vital to me, I learn about myself and others through writing. It is so necessary. The sharing, the "goodness" is an afterthought. And I also want to be a good writer. I feel numb writing this out, shame, deep deep self-protection.

Breathe. Self-compassion. Crossroads. And joy in knowing myself, my fears my struggles. I am alive, human. Perhaps that is what I am interested in writing a book about, how to accept myself, ourselves as human.

Again fog, vulnerability. Not about writing a book. Sharing this vulnerable voice. The class last week told me it is a gift I have to offer. It is where I feel most alive, whole, when I am learning about what hurts me, confuses me, excites me. Writing to learn, to know, to embrace, to love.

Not to be perfect, nor to wow them, to show what a brilliant poet I am. To be alive, to sing out, to connect. A new way to see what my one-woman-shows are about. My own self-exploration. Teaching others to do the same, to engage with their own stories, challenges, demons. To take care of themselves through words, to grow into being whole, embracing light and shadow.

LYNDA

What I most want from our time together first and foremost is to WRITE, to go to the page in the quiet of our pens moving over paper to do for ten minutes or half an hour what I love to do—which is be on this blank page with my heart, soul, creativity, mood, vision and in the midst of daily life—work, kids, etc.—I love knowing that time is protected in my calendar to come together with beautiful writing soul sisters, the two of you specifically, and write. I am honouring my passion for writing by giving it time and space and community. This is my highest need for our time together at this one moment in my life—a moment in my life when I can exhale and say "Yes, I am here, I am writing, I am listening and loving your words too"—to write, read, be heard, be validated—Yes, Yes, Yes!

I have enough places in my life right now that have deadlines and to-do lists and deliverables—I don't particularly feel called to that here. I would love to just BE in this exquisite community of passionate women writers—journal writers and beyond into our public writing goals—for this to be a place for cheerleading those goals, to be the shared wind beneath our writing wings.

I want our time together to be FUN, inspiring, empowering, supportive and celebrating of us as three women who write, three women who bring writing to others in our own unique ways. I love the sharing of the writing we do when together because I value to hold onto that exquisite, fresh, raw and real part of ourselves we offer for glimpse and embrace in our time together. Who knows, maybe the collection of these spontaneous pieces becomes our book—a sampling of women's voices, our voices, uncensored and captured in print—just because.

I need this to be my one time in a week, or a month, that I know I will write with sacred whimsy, in that I feel complete. I trust our book, *Writing Alone Together*, to be born like all new life in the perfect timing, when the gestation period has been long enough for lungs to breathe outside this writing womb we are creating together.

WENDY

Communion, connection, listening, sharing, depth, not only surface. Encouragement, enticement to go to the places I need to go to be true to my core, which as a writer means writing about what I need to write about, to discover my self through the process. To be engaged in my writing, even when I don't feel I know the way or am unwilling to risk the pain or uncertainty or the obstacles seem too great.

I know I'm not as ambitious as either of you are, in terms of my goals for publishing and production. I am a procrastinator. And I have fantasies—of each of us creating writing circles with other women—perhaps together or separately. Making magic happen with other women on our island. Sharing fantasies feels exciting, life-affirming and open-heart-oriented.

At this stage of my life I crave connection. Our lives, our writing, our commonalities, our differences—these are all elements which excite and enrich my life.

2. Right Now/Write Now

When in the act of writing, I fully entrust myself to it: place myself willingly in the very midst of the beautiful chaos of meaning unfolding. The terror and joy of this are like none other. Writing is a way of perceiving where everything converges. Which is possibly eternity.

—BETSY WARLAND

We start from this moment. We have said this before and we will probably say it again, because it is so vital to what we are doing here. No matter what we write about, nor what style we write in, starting from this moment is what happens. No matter where we are located, what kind of notebook or journal or laptop we write in, we start right here, in this moment. We pick up the pen or pencil and place them on the page or our fingers on the keyboard, take a few breaths (which we may not even be aware of). We assume the "write" position, whatever it is. All of this happens in this moment, the only one there is.

What a gift this practice is. Spiritual teachers like the Dalai Lama, Eckhart Tolle and Pema Chodron advise us again and again to be in the moment, to show up fully here. And that is what we do, before we even begin to write the words down. We arrive. We bring our bodies and minds and hearts and souls right here. We land in this very moment, with all of our senses, our feelings, our thoughts and we begin.

Instead of trying to make our experience a certain way, or to control, adjust, or fix it, we simply rest in the awareness of whatever is here. We do not have to do anything about it except to become curious about what is happening.

Journal Writing Prompt

Feel yourself sitting on the cushion, the chair, the floor or wherever you are. Take a breath and then another one, smell what you smell, hear what you hear, feel what you feel. With this awareness, begin with the words:

Right now _____.

82

LYNDA

Right now I am trying to give myself permission to keep moving my pen across this page when my baby needs me to feed him—so patient, gurgling, eating his own hands, using every coo, oh, aw that he has available to him so far. This morning we went to aqua fit—up at 6 a.m., then the routine—breakfast, pack Jackson's lunch, read stories, dance, scramble eggs, arrange childcare to come an hour early to make the class possible, carpool, pick up Heidi, take her on errands, get to the pool, jump in the water, feel it wash over my unbathed self, the music loud but not audible in the hollow of the pool surroundings, until the song YMCA belts out and we all splash and jump spelling this song in the air with our arms. I look over to Jesse and see him calling for me with his lips wide open, crying, only I can't hear him with fifteen splashing fitness buffs. I get out of the water five minutes after class starts, nurse him chlorine at the side of the pool, wet his clothes against my body, try to set him back down to no avail, $6 for class, $20 extra for childcare, and two hours out of the morning and I spelled YMCA. I change, dry—Jesse and me—sit on the floor between a garbage pail and a bench press and I nurse my baby boy, being with the only NOW there is. And now, me here still, still and quiet in the embrace of pen, paper and women who I so hold space for in my heart and in my dreams as we take our writing and ourselves forward—right now!

AHAVA

Right now write now this is my time although I have to say it's all my time, everything I am doing and my butt on the chair, breathing in, Jesse breathes too, tension in my shoulders, the weight of it, all that needs to get done. I feel a smile coming on—beautiful music beautiful women beautiful breathing baby. I let my pen go slow, no need to rush. I take my time here, a kind of headache, a body sigh, the mind invited to stillness, resists.

Oh to feel my lover's arms around me tonight, to finally let go into his embrace, surrender achievement, out there striving, give myself over to pleasure at his hands, mouth, tongue, remember that part of me who loves to dance between the sheets with him, who welcomes his affection, attention, how he knows where to lay his hands on me for genuine healing, how he has learned to give what I through my life have come to need, the kind of touch, the tease.

Out in the world I get pleasure from so many things and then he is left alone to dream himself. Tonight I come back to loving him for I have loved myself enough this week, this month. Tonight I rest, receive the love of someone else, let go of ambition, decisions. And now and now the tears have cleansed.

WENDY

Right now, meeting in my playroom, I am submerging the rather sour green grape into my mouth. Jesse's grunts, cries, utterances filling the space. Three comfortable pads for our *tuchases*. Fun and cozy and full of anticipation.

My life flows here and there. As strange as it all seems, with the months, years, decades whizzing along, almost past, I am content. When I wrap myself around Corrie's soft and beautiful body, morning wake-up kisses with Rosey dog, perpetual purrs of Iris and just the everyday aspects of this life I am living, I note this contentment somewhere in my psyche, as well as the dissonant, challenging, difficult times and events. But I feel more determined to honour the sweetness rather than dwell on the pain.

The fragility of life sometimes weighs down on me. I am acutely aware of the preciousness of it all, this life. And I know that at any moment darkness, illness, abrupt changes, death can implode upon this life I have created. Illusionary, illusive as it all is, best-laid plans, dreams and fantasies, desires, bucket lists. I know it's all subject to change and even destruction. All the final "nos" that take lives, dreams, plans and nullify them.

So I want to be here in this very moment as much as possible. Being this me who writes, prints, in this journal of stark white pages with thin, black pilot pen poised just so on the paper. My fingers holding this pen are beginning to ache, tingling, and it's time to stop, for now, knowing I can always return.

3. Embodiment

Deep writing emerges from the space between the inhalation and exhalation, that space in between the doing and the dreaming, our place of power, of mystery, and of authenticity.

—LARAINE HERRING

What if writing were a simple, significant yet necessary way to achieve spiritual, emotional, and psychic whole-

ness?...What if writing were as important and as a basic human function and as significant to maintaining and promoting our psychic and physical wellness as, say, exercise, healthful food, pure water, clean air, rest and repose, and some soul-satisfying practice?

—LOUISE DESALVO

Our bodies, these physical forms we are in, support us in so many ways. Yet most of us take our physical bodies for granted, until we are ill, injured or aging, and then are forced to pay more attention. Our bodies work in relationship with the other dimensions of the self—including our minds, hearts and spirits. Journal writing is a physical act—it involves moving the pen over the page or typing at a computer—the hands, fingers, wrists, arms, shoulders, the whole body is involved. This provides the opportunity to embody our writing.

Journal Writing Prompt

Go for a walk, to an exercise class or engage in some other form of physical activity together. After you finish, write together or bring to awareness the experience of some physical activity. Before you start writing, close your eyes, connect with your breath, notice your inhale and your exhale. Let your body have a voice on the page.

WENDY

Why haven't I relished her more all these years? Grateful for her flexibility, litheness, abilities to move quickly, stretch deeply, muscles at my disposal, intuitive movements between movements. There have always been bodily experiences that have frightened me or that I simply could not accomplish—like hanging up-side down, doing somersaults in the water, hanging on bars, or anything having to do with heights. And my own natural gifts or bodily resources—like my flexible hips, easy outward rotation of my legs and agility with speed and executing quick feet and leg motions—have served me well.

Corrie, my partner, relishes my body, even my belly. She says I'm sexy, that my skin is so soft. But I would not say I have truly appreciated the gifts of my body and I am ever aware of this as time passes and I recognize more limitations and sources of discomfort. I would urge all of us to worship these physical temples we have been given, not take for granted our strengths. And at the same time I know how much movement and physical health are valued and coveted in our culture. None of us want to admit that we will, or may, eventually lose our physical abilities or even moving our limbs. I've heard of athletes and dancers who were paralyzed or who gradually lost control of their bodies.

Control of my body—ballet was the vehicle for me to exercise and produce this control. These bodies of ours are great teachers; we are continually teachers and learners, explorers and discoverers, pushing against discomfort, widening the boundaries and also accepting limitations. Yoga shows me how to be in balance with all the parts of my self. How to both push and accept and ultimately surrender to the unknown. To be grounded in the earth and reach up towards the sky. To assume poses that resemble animals I almost never see but I know are alive and part of the same universe I inhabit. To find those deeply satisfying stretches that extend and allow my limbs to open and release. To honour my quite small movement and not take myself beyond the point of pain. To confront the critic within and the helpful coach. And at the end of class, to assume the corpse pose, to practice the ultimate letting go and surrender. To have gratitude for the practice and trust in the process, to let myself just be. Many similarities to writing practice.

LYNDA

I am moving forward as a mother, soon to wean my youngest, reclaiming this part of my body—not shared. I have been feeding babies from my breasts for three years—never a day or a night that my boobs have not been taken out from beneath clothing, suckled, touched, pinched, hit, grabbed, bit—small hands resting splayed, holding me to his lips—directing my flesh for his nutrients and needs.

What will it be like to have my body back? To once again offer this part of me to my husband without cheerios and sticky fingers patterned on my skin—to replace the easy off flannels that have allowed easy access for nursing at 1, 2, 3, 4 a.m.—night after night. To drop soft silk over my body—feel my root chakra hungry. Moving, stretching, running, sweating, strong, flexible, balanced, whole, honoured—to love my body—to fully accept the way it carries me through daily life, the way it waits for me from time to time to show up fully, the way it forgives me, urges me, supports me—calls me forth now into my best physical form so far—this body always loved by a strong mind, loving heart and connected spirit—introducing me to parts of myself I discover as new over and over again. The way this body speaks—a gentle whisper, a loud cry, the stories it tells on the page and in silence—the body a source of wisdom, intuition—a wise guide on this journey—always waiting to be invited in more fully to the splendour of each breath, a sparkling diamond of pure white light—created with a finger print held by no one else on this planet—unique, necessary, part of all that is.

I learned yesterday that Sue, my friend and card-making inspiration, left this physical plane. Cancer attacked her body after a year of chemo, Mexican healers, oncologists, eating right, sitting still, surrendering, fighting. She died peacefully with her two grown children—her son and daughter—and her husband at her bedside. She will be cremated tomorrow—her bones and skin, her smiling face and sparkling eyes will turn to ashes, be put in a pot, sit on a mantle—a body no longer, a life only memory can touch.

I want to move and dance and sing and play and write—because I can! To show up fully each and every day with the full awareness that someday my eyes, my smile, my belly, my life will be ashes in the urn—already crafted by a local artist—already sitting high up on the shelf, pottery for now, decorating our kitchen. Later it will hold a soft grey ash memory of all this good living, of this body here, now, holding this pen, moving it across this blank white page called my life.

AHAVA

On the floor of Lynda's beautiful handmade studio surrounded by books, blankets and barely audible scratching of pens we sit and rest after our workout together at Fulford Hall. We sit together, write together each in her own journal with her own pen, jotting down her own thoughts feelings, sensations, memories. We sit barefoot and socked, in scarves, vests, jeans and cotton pants. We sit with our backs straight or leaning into soft support. Breathing and writing.

I sit and my body rests, relaxes, hands are active—left hand gripping the top of my journal as right hand scratches these curves, lines, marks—a task I have been participating in for almost thirty-eight years, I imagine. This *languaging.* Is it the body's language, these words? Would the body speak differently if I asked it to? Who is doing the writing? My hand? Heart? Mind?

My body speaks, sometimes in practised practical ways, other times anxious and frantic, out of necessity and/or propensity to stop pause prop itself up and pay attention.

I spend so much time on the farm now I wonder if my body is different when I leave, something about the trees, flowers, barn and spa building, lilies in the pond, horses in the pasture. Those intricate wooden gates I open and close unleashing metal feet, pulling back wooden levers. Everywhere on the farm there are gates. To enter one space and leave another I must unclasp a metal prong, undo a chain link cable, unwrap it from around a post.

Is the farm a new body I live within? Do I write there now, in that body? A larger container for my words, wishes and wants? I look out my window as if through wider eyes, trees are new farm-mates, a new circle of friends. No wonder I felt sad when I didn't see the horses in the field yesterday. Although they have only been pasturing here for a few weeks, they have taken up residence in this larger body of mine. They are new limbs, appendages or is it only the heart that grows wide enough to house all these new companions? Like the story of the Buddhist monk who upon being asked by a visitor why he was going around naked in his little house, responded that the whole world is his trousers. Seeing the farm as my body expands my understanding of what it means to be alive; how caring for the earth is like caring for my own flesh.

4. I Am Called

Writing saved my life. Before I found writing I had exhausted all the other ways of being in the world that I knew about. But, as with anything that one makes entirely one's own, I had to reinvent writing. I had to unravel everything I had been taught and wind it back up again, my way.

—GAIL SHER

So often in our lives we are moving from one act of doing to the next. We do not pause to check in with ourselves, to listen for what is calling us, to what is drawing our attention. The journal can be a place to open to inspiration, listen closely for whatever or whoever is calling. These callings might be heard and known through the drama of our dreams, the heat of our desires, the joy of our inspiration or the anxiety in our anticipation of what's to come. Feeling called is a gift as it gives us the opportunity to respond with our bodies, minds and hearts. Our callings align us with our most authentic participation in creating and healing the world.

Where do you feel called to pay attention in your life at this time? Are you listening?

Journal Writing Prompt

LYNDA

I feel drawn to energies that are alive, upbeat, infused with passion, interest, reflection and revolution small and large. I hold an image of the three sister mountains in my mind's eye—large stone reaching skyward, rock solid, years of holding strong in this one spot, this one place upon the earth. Three sisters…we are three sisters, reaching upward for places of wisdom, knowing and strength through writing and dialogue. We are strong. We are women who write, think, wonder and reflect. We shape knowledge for ourselves and others. We get curious about one another, our experiences, and the world we live in.

While sleep would not come to me in the dark of last night, I went to the computer and typed, words falling out of me onto the only light available in the room— the blank screen. An hour passed and I went back to bed with my mind alert, turned on the light and started reading the words put to paper by someone else. Words, ideas, words, mine, yours, night, day, light, dark, sleep, sleeplessness. Moments after I turned out the light, feeling sleep very near, the blankets soft against my shoulders and neck, tucking in close to Pedro's warm skin, drifting, drifting, then Jesse's cry fills the space between being awake and falling asleep. I go to him, nurse him, rock him, his eyes remain open, he sits up and says "lamb," bringing his stuffed animal in for a hug. "Blue bear" another hug. I hold him close, say "Good night Jess, it is still night time, go to sleep my lovey." "Lamb, blue bear," he repeats. I surrender to his wakefulness and my own discomfort and chill, sitting in his room and carry him to our bed. Two thirty, three o'clock, three thirty nursing, flip flopping, no sleep.

Now here in the light of day I feel the fog of last night's sleeplessness, while also feeling the aliveness of our wide-ranging insights. Insights, that is in part what our book project is about for me. Learning, my learning and thinking and articulating the juice of this passion called writing. Writing in the mountains, writing in the middle of the night, writing in my journal, writing as craft, writing memoir, writing as a healing art, writing as voice, writing as a way of knowing... writing by hand, by finger strokes up this keyboard, writing in my mind when both paper and computer are someplace else, writing life while living it.

WENDY

My heart strings tug as I reveal (to you?) (to me?) my connections to close women friends who are far away. Pulled into anxiety, fear, trepidation—depression. Taking precedence over any of my own writing or teaching projects, funneling into a tunnel that resides at the pit of my belly, then shoots into my heart, my chest— up and back down again.

WHAT AM I CALLED TO DO? TO WRITE? TO EXPRESS? If I listen, LISTEN to my self, I can tell how obsessed I have become with L's unknown illness, with H's upcoming surgery, with the economic disaster (isn't that what they—the ruling hierarchy—want us to believe?). BREATHE. IN AND OUT. WRITE ABOUT IT. TAKE THE TIME. GO INSIDE.

I do not want to think about or believe she has B cancer. I do not want to think about cancer at all!

HOW AM I IMPACTED?

This feels too close, my inner circle, my kin. My family of closest women friends. My resistance does not help L, nor myself. I feel powerless. I am powerless. I feel unmotivated, ungrounded, undisciplined. How to function, to even appreciate life when it all feels so fragile, so vulnerable, so fraught with dis-ease, sadness, despair and fear.

I FEAR—this separation between us. The gulf between the haves and have nots. Between those who will be the most impacted by this supposed "economic downturn." Anger at a system that does so little to actually support people in their lives.

Reading *Hope Dies Last* (by Studs Terkel) has been a gift with its stories of people maintaining faith and hope and well being despite struggles of poverty, displacement, inhumane treatment, injustice, the brutalities of discrimination in its myriad forms.

DO I TRUST IN THIS PROCESS?

CAN THIS WRITING HEAL ME?

DO I HAVE HOPE?

WILL WE SURVIVE?

IS THIS YET ANOTHER OPPORTUNITY TO RECOGNIZE THE IMPERMANENCE OF LIFE? A REASON TO LOVE EVEN MORE FEROCIOUSLY?

I catch my self wondering about my self.

Watching. Wondering. Am I a joyful person? Do I bring openheartedness to others? Am I available? In sensing my own limitations, I realize there's internal work to do, ways I can, if I choose to, bring out more internal graciousness, receptivity and joy into my being. I know it's there, but I have been unable to access it. Always more to investigate, to perceive. I feel vague and disengaged, disconnected, disassociated with my core, my power, my wholeness. MURKY. Almost waves of nausea. Is this just the freedom, the privilege of choice? That I have the opportunity to choose my tasks more now than ever?

AHAVA

I want the wildness, love the way life happens to me or is it I am the living, or I am life. I love the witnessing of life as it is happening. I am interested in some kind of taming actually. I have to admit that. I have been writing to tame the demons in my own head, those voices I grew up believing about not being enough or about being a girl in this way and that to please the guy or my mother or society's ideal of what it means to be a girl. I write to tame the judgment, the prejudice, so when I look at another who is different than me, I choose acceptance and honouring rather than criticism or shunning. I write to tame the nervous energy, the monkey mind that makes me feel as if I am totally out of control and have no handle on my life and the way I am living it.

Both the wildness and the taming are precious, the way we encounter one another, how we listen and protect and nourish one another here in this circle of journal writing, how we are becoming used to the role of witness, how we hurray for our successes and acknowledge our grief for the loss of ways we have been in the world because we three are each getting older. And how we leave room for the conversation that emerges between us, each offering a voice in, and then something happens—the books we are reading, the inspiration we bring, each of us continuing to fight her own fight for the stories that want to live through us, the liberation we bear in bellies and thighs and minds, for all women and all children and all lovers, gay and straight. We are taming one another, learning to listen to the wildness and to make it into memoir and glory as we unfold the larger story of this circle of three.

So the meeting of wilderness and civilization, the edge where the liminal and personal and political merge, the bridge this whole world stumbles onto day after day as it carries on living, working and loving and the wars we all would like to see end. But we have to end them all first inside ourselves. And that is what the stories do, the pens scratching are truces written in blood and effort for our pain and our struggling to make meaning, to see some light of salvation, to be lifted up even as the wounded lie on the battleground, their ink dried up, colour drained from their faces, the map fading where there once were veins and a heartbeat. We, too, will pass away, while drummer and flute player continue into the next generation. The storytellers were the ones who sat around the fire and told the tales of the day, keeping the village soul alive through the words and images woven through smoke and around benches, under blankets and between the grip of fingers holding onto the ones they love.

We sit here in this warm cozy space and for three hours at a time we take up our seats on the rim of the fire, we hold our voices firm and we steady our limbs, rocking to and fro as if the whole island were an infant in our arms. We wade into the news of the season, we make room for the breath of fir and cedar, for the dirt in each of our garden plots to seed and sprout into new stories, food for thought and contemplation and taming all the doubt and fear and anger and frustration and joy and unknowing.

We are three women on the edge of the circle. We stand here and hold the thread of the heavens in one hand, the needle of the earth in the other. We weave them into stories, making it whole again over and over with each telling. We weave stories for birth and stories for dying, stories for betrayal and for reunion, stories for all the joys and sorrows of our lives. And we leave room for those stories yet to be told.

5. Quotations

Often I am asked, who taught me how to write? Every-thing, I want to say. Everything taught me, everything became my teacher, though at the time I was not aware of all the tender shoots that helped me along.

—NATALIE GOLDBERG

As the three of us have shared our passion for jour-nalling, we have noticed how often we are inspired by the words of other writers. Each of us is not only a writer but an avid, dedicated reader and thus we have accumulated favourite quotes from favourite authors on writing and feminism and self-care and healthy re-lationships and teaching love in the world. The inspi-ration of others is another way to gain access to the truth(s) of our own experience. Bravo, we call out in our circle when we appreciate the beauty, depth or clarity evoked in one of our entries or those in a quote shared by a sister.

Choose and write from:

Journal Writing Prompt

- **a favourite quote you've come across by an au-thor you like**
- **a few words or phrase from one of your sister journal writers**
- **a word or phrase from a previous writing**
- **one of the quotes in this book that inspires you**
- **one of the following quotes**

**"An empty page in your journal is an invitation."
—Stephanie Dowrick**

"The moment, the whole moment, and nothing but the moment." —Stephen Nachmanovitch

"Doing the work of love requires resisting the status quo."—bell hooks

"If you could see yourself, how could you help loving yourself?"—Helene Cixous

AHAVA

"Many a false step was made by standing still."

—Ancient Chinese proverb

When I first read the quote I wondered if it had something to tell me about the seven-day meditation retreat set to start on Saturday that I am to attend, feeling excited while also anxious. A retreat of silence, attention drawing inward toward self, a respite before the hectic pace of living in Vancouver for three months this fall beginning in September.

And yet there's the question: a week of meditation and no words. Would it be better spent in meditation on my own words, in action, pursuing the CD? That is the question. Is this quote about being true to myself and honouring my creations and acknowledging what false step I may be about to take? Or is it a false quote and is my true north the week away from everything? The CD will wait another week.

What is this fear of jumping in, just doing it? I deserve this and so does the world. And oh the trees they hold their branches out and gesture to me, welcome home, our sister, we have been waiting for you, it is good to have you home.

WENDY

"The important thing is this: to be able to at any moment sacrifice what we are for what we could become."

—CHARLES DUBOIS

To sacrifice what we are..........to *not* sacrifice what we are.

Sacrifice was presented to me as something parents do for children, as explanation of the gargantuan re-sponse-abilities parenting requires. I always felt loved, cared for and about, protected and pretty safe. I didn't know that my side of the assumed bargain was for my sacrifice as their child—not only to express my love for their devotion and attentiveness and protection, but for me to serve as their sacrificial lamb as I was expect-ed to surrender my own identity—my needs, wants, desires, my self in search for who exactly I am—and replace that with someone who would be able to pay them back for their sacrifices.

Now this was not an easy task to accomplish—the erasure of self and re-molding, renovating necessary to either become a different self or present the appear-ance of a new (or actually perceived as previous) self. And I know strict adherence to self is dangerous, as the quote implies in the ways it can restrict one's ex-periences and individual selves. But this world, these cultures that don't exactly reward us for straying from the norm, is simply not life-affirming. I have empathy for disappointment and heartache that comes from one's children, spouse, partner, even friends straying from past identities. I mourn the loss of Sandra (after her death and even before), my first woman lover and our pleasure, connection, sisterhood.

And perhaps the importance is in each of us allowing ourselves to be as fully ourselves as we can, however that feels, however we are being or becoming. As I
poured my own compassion and comprehension into
who I sensed myself becoming, I trusted others would
allow me this passage as well: to not sacrifice my own
needs and desires in the hopes that others would never
have to sacrifice themselves or any vital part of their
being.

LYNDA

*"The goal of life is to make your heartbeat match the beat
of the universe, to match your nature with Nature."*

—JOSEPH CAMPBELL

What is my nature? My pulse quickening with anticipation feeling called forward to something not quite
known in my life. Feeling called, period. Each direction
I turn—north, south, east, west—I hear the same message and invitation from the universe: use your gifts,
talents, experience to be in service to those who…I'm
stopping here. Jesse cries. He needs something now.
Not in twelve minutes when our timed writing is done
but now.

Each day I am moving between dreaming, design-
ing my next professional steps and Now. Now I feed
my baby, don't get a diaper on him in time, get peed
on my hand, my pant leg, the phone rings and rings,
our home line, work line, I answer, I ignore depending. I recite ABC's, teach colours, play counting games.
Last night Jackson and I painted. I opened the green
first, then red, then blue and I watched him notice the
colours mixing—red and blue becoming purple—his

eyes lighting up seeing his own magic on paper as he squealed "purple, purple" and I tried to explain the mixing of one colour with another to yet another. He wiped green paint on his pyjama top while I spoke hearing my words drift into this beautiful silence between us, painting, playing, being.

Sleeping, awake, sleeping, awake again—that is the nature of things now. I just fall asleep and Jesse's awake for another feed. I hold him to my breast propped by pillows, untangling my arm from the mosquito nets hanging over our bed. Pedro reaches to hold my hand under the covers, searches and rests his hand on my leg and I hear him breathe himself to sleep. I'm awake and one by one my boys sleep. I walk into the kitchen and there over Fulford Harbour the near full moon, a huge pumpkin in the sky, winking at me in the darkness. With my eyes wide open I stare back at nature, hold her round, voluptuous image clearly in my own shadow cast on the wall. I walk back to bed, fall asleep with moon in my memory. Safe, loved, loving and on the edge of my dream about far away travels. Jesse stirs again, this time I roll left offering mama juices to his wanting belly. Somewhere between hunger and satisfaction, we sleep.

The nature of myself is transforming. There is a self I know—this body, this woman who was me before having babies—and now there is this other self—naturally, mother. Mother naturally. Nature. The nature of this mother self, peeking into and past the full moon, hungry and satiated all at once. I walk over slippery seaweed collecting shells with my son and we giggle picking up small crabs. We are together, nature in human form, loving each other, loving ourselves.

6. Passion Statement

Just as we have a critic on one shoulder, we have an angel on the other, whose only goal is to help our writing take on its greatness. It does this by wooing us to our passion.

———Janet O. Hagberg

A passion statement is like your own personal mantra, a slice of your life purpose or your soul purpose. Or just you, putting words on top of one another or beside one another on the page. You will know what you need and want to say. If you don't know, just start moving your pen across the paper and let your knowing reveal itself word by word. Follow your intuition, choose a form that feels right to you. That's what we did when we wrote the passion statements below.

Journal Writing Prompt

Write your own passion statement. What deeply matters most to you, fuels your writing and your life? What feels alive and nourishing and invigorating? What aligns you to your true self? Let yourself play, free-associate, riff. Sing out sisters!

WENDY

Writing in a journal has always
been my passion
writing in a journal
alone, myself
words on paper
it started that way
later, after reading Anaïs and Simone
a black blank book

black ink
no lines
refuge for my heart, my soul
my burgeoning awareness
as a girl turning woman
a hippie turning feminist
turning lesbian
a middle-class Jew
turning socialist–feminist
turning, turning away
charting my turns
my moments etched in ink
of many colours and shapes
accompanying me along my journeys
pathways, doorways, movements
when lover-less something
to come home to
when partnered
a place
to turn to my self
in large groups and meetings
a time to centre
in large demonstrations and actions
a way to take notice of history-in-the-making
in times of distress
holding me close
in joyous rapture
a way to re-member
the presence of the ecstatic
connecting me to my simultaneous
experience of past and present
infusing my aliveness with
some certitude in the
shifts and changing patterns
sheltering me from fixed

notions of what to expect
enriching and reinvigorating and infusing
my life, my days, my nights
my heart, my body, my soul
with wonder.

AHAVA

THIS IS MY HEART
This is my kissing ground
of being, dancing swell
of presence

a mouth to mouth incantation
celebration, elucidation

This is my feet on floor,
sky on mind
bellowing forward
to write so our rights count
counting on me to be writer healer

This is my bright timing
letting go and moving forward
a shock of red shoes delivering happy

This is my feverish mountain
gypsy jewish buddhist
boogie soul

This is my wandering ink
belted-OUT voice
an unabashed conviction
(m)other-load *sans enfants*

my exquisite expression
and invigorating rhythm
a prayer story narrative envisioning
a favourite key to unlocking vision

as my tongue swirls
lips smack into truth

a darling handshaking caress
gorgeous limitless edition

This is my fed-up silence
fiddling on the roof of my tongue
a sound of believing in love
an empty caress of air against
a vociferous plate of adjectives

my virtual plumbline
of question still unanswered

This is my time to want, to have
to need, better yet, almost

I am only
just Beginning.

LYNDA

words tumbling
from heart
found in memory
from this day
or yesterday
dreaming tomorrow

pay attention
to your life
to each other's lives

gentle, quiet
still
silence
solitude

knowing yourself, with love

window, peer into
your soul
rain drops sing
deer visit
you are not
just visiting
your life
arrive FULLY
sweet dancer
somersault JOY
around and around

SING
out loud
laugh, giggle
your bliss
so others can hear

so you can
hear
blessed woman

of the earth
stone, sand, water
wind

Fire, find your fire
hot, touch, steamy
alive on flames

Belly, heart
what's in your
green chakra?

intuition,
listen carefully
within

woman you know
yourself
Best of all.

All or nothing?
everything
say Yes, Now, to everything

Know deeply
pulse, leaf, garden
of mine
seed in soil
reaching down and up
at once
for sun, dirt

Your life,
my life—
together spinning
stillness
around.

7. The Road Not Taken

Two roads diverged in a wood...And I, I took the road less traveled by, and that has made all the difference.

—ROBERT FROST

Journal therapy (the use of journal writing to know the self) is a bridge into first our own humanity, and then our own spirituality. The road stretches out before us, and our ultimate task is the journey.

—KATHLEEN ADAMS

The Road Not Taken releases us from the limitations of our true-to-life stories, encouraging us to reimagine the events of our lives. We revisit choices we've made and explore the what-ifs. We return to some of our defining moments and explore what could have happened. We can approach this with seriousness or with humour. Through "trying on" alternative stories, we depart from the actual events and feel what it might have been like to walk a different path.

There is something very expansive about writing from this prompt. We can imagine experiences we never had, have craved or wondered about. We can contemplate our most significant choices or events. We can return to painful moments, difficult losses and regrets. And we can transform these as we write something new. We can try on different tones and styles. We can exaggerate and fantasize, follow our impulses and experiment with possibilities, allowing ourselves this time to take another road.

We credit Ira Progroff, creator of *The Intensive Journal*, for this prompt.

Reflect on a significant time in your life—an event, choice or change—and write as if something else happened. Write about a road you did not take...

Journal Writing Prompt

LYNDA

I want to go back to the morning after the night before and the night before that and the morning. I want to return to the moment in the dark, in the forest, when I had only your damp hand leading the way. I want to go back to the smell of smoke and the crackling bonfire and the sound of the Tragically Hip blaring from your truck and the taste of rum and beer that mixed when I wished your lips found mine—near the old spruce tree outside of your bedroom window, again on the living room floor with the lumpy mattress and the musty sleeping bag hiding us from the party in the woods now well beyond.

I kept pulling away, the truth, the gold band with the solitary diamond in my jean pocket. I had to tell you the truth. I know I said it was just going to be "a break" when you drove away in May. I remember your rearview brake lights, still. Sometime between putting your truck in reverse and the start of university in September, I fell in love with someone else. I knew him for many years. I fell fast and secured it tight with a wedding date and a promise of forever with the ring—the ring now off my left finger, rubbing against my right hip as I press against you on the floor—getting ready to push you away, for good.

I thought I would forget about you, the smell of your skin, the shape of your Spock ear, the sound of your belly laugh and the feel of your fingertips tracing my body. I have not forgotten. You are my road not taken, not once, but twice.

AHAVA

She kicks her feet
across the sand

her blonde curls dance
through sunlight,

shakes her barely four-year-old
self along the beach.

Other kids play
beside her but
she doesn't seem
to notice.

Her hands trail along
water's crooked edge
catch kelp and tiny
shimmer fish,
let them
go.

I watch her play, start to cry,
sunglasses fog, wonder
how life would be
without her.

He surprises her, crouches
to see what new joy
she's found.

Now they walk
toward me, two sparkling
pearls.

WENDY

She never really felt like an academic, but she found herself in school a lot. School was liberating. "The best decision she ever made," she used to say. Naïve, inexperienced, shy, sex-less, she needed to escape the confines of L.A. and her parents' liberal yet restrictive enclave to truly experience herself, discover who she was.

Santa Cruz seemed like a likely enough place to flee to, after the heart-wrenching break-up with Sandra, her first love. Tired of running into her, her new lover and their two dogs at street intersections, all three dogs (hers and theirs) excitedly cavorting for the brief moments it took to cross the street, living within three blocks of each other, she sent in her application to the "consciousness" doctoral program, hoping to be selected.

After years of activism and radical socialist–feminist organizing, she donned the academic identity. It was hard at first separating herself from the collectives she used to be involved in, but gradually she began to take to the ways it offered her entrance into the inner sanctums she had so detested. Invited to seminars and teas and late night chats with professors and other academics-in-training, she discovered it began to suit her. Assuming the authority it conferred upon her, she shed her old politics like old hippy attire, even shaved her underarms and hairy legs for the occasion, donned a new, shorter coif and threw away old phone books.

Years passed before she realized she had stopped writing in her journal, useful no longer. Her identity finally merged within academia. She stopped writing about subjects that mattered to her, because her advi-

sors warned her against trying anything a bit too con-
troversial. She became one of the swarms of competi-
tive academics-in-training, salivating for that scarce of
all acquisitions: a university professorship.

8. Words We Do Not Have

*What are the words you do not yet have? What do you
need to say? What are the tyrannies you swallow day by
day and attempt to make your own, until you will sicken
and die of them, still in silence?*

—AUDRE LORDE

*Allow yourself to go into forbidden territory and explore
as far as you are able. Write what you do not want to
write. Write what you believe is of interest to no one.
Write what you cannot tell your closest friend or your
spouse or your child or your partner.*

—NINA WISE

There are times in our writing and in our lives when
something might be difficult to communicate, express
or even remember. It could be a certain topic, circum-
stance, memory. Instead of being fearful or resistant,
we can allow ourselves the freedom to give voice to
these challenging experiences within the pages of our
journals. This may feel scary or painful even, but the
release that can come from acknowledging feelings is
worth it.

Journal Writing Prompt **What are the words you do not have? What can you
not write about?**

WENDY

I was diagnosed with breast cancer just before my partner and I moved from our home in Oregon and relocated to Salt Spring Island. It was during the beginning of what was to be my last semester teaching women's studies at Portland State University. After one month of classes, a tumour was detected in a mammogram and my entire life was changed forever. One month after that, I had surgery which removed the tumour and two lymph nodes, which at first were seen as completely clear but, after closer inspection, one node had a microscopic amount of cancer, which made my cancer stage two. I began a course of radiation for thirty-three treatments. During that time I went on sick-leave from teaching, getting almost all of my monthly salary (which had accumulated during the many years I was teaching), fortunately had high-quality medical insurance which covered the bulk of my enormous medical bills, received regular acupuncture and shiatsu treatments and saw a counsellor. We put our house on the market and sold it in three weeks, packed up our belongings, gave away and got rid of lots (mostly my books, papers and collections I had saved for twenty-some years) and moved to our home on Salt Spring Island, just days before my fifty-fourth birthday. Strangely enough, we followed the plans we had initially created regarding our timeline for moving, but obviously had not anticipated my getting breast cancer. Ahava and I started meeting six months later.

I can't write about:

SELF HATRED.
HATING MY LIFE.

HATING MY CHOICES.
HATING MY BODY.
HATING MY FRIENDS.

I won't tell you how utterly amazing my life is, how in awe I am for these beautiful surroundings, the view of the ocean when I arise, the sunrise, my lover's graceful countenance, her slim sexiness, the feel of her skin moving against mine.

HATING MY BROTHER. HATING MY MOTHER. HATING CANCER.

I cannot admit how utterly grateful I am that my beloved adores my belly. I do not share her adoration. I would like nothing better than for it to be less fleshy, flatter, firmer.

HATING HOW WORTHLESS I FEEL AT TIMES.

HATING FEAR AND HOW IT TAKES HOLD.

HATING HOW I TURN AGAINST SHE WHO IS CLOSEST AND DEAREST TO ME.

Afraid of admitting how joyful and truly marvelous this life is only to feel so at odds with it, when I feel pain or the fear of cancer returning.

HATING CANCER IN ALL ITS MANIFESTATIONS.

HATING THE INDUSTRY THAT FIGHTS AGAINST CANCER.

HATING PINK RIBBONS AND RUNS FOR LIFE AND SHAVED HEADS AND THAT CHEMOTHERAPY SHIT!

AHAVA

Look at them in the trees
chittering, scattered

Look how she's left them

tossed them some hard bread
a few blankets for warmth

sent them out to beg,
their wings paper thin, koan-like

Look how she struggles with their flying
each more flagrant
lifting their tails to show the scars

Look at them singing
their sad, blessed oratorios to a
hopeful sky

they stare at her shivering

invite her into their holy
resonance of bark
and air

LYNDA

What can I not write about? What words don't I have
yet? What I can't write about is screaming loudly from
my belly, through my heart, and rattling my brain into
a headache, a vice grip of silence. It is not mine to say,
it is his story, his news, his history. But it is my story,
too. It wasn't a secret because it was never known until
recently. Now that it is known, and been spoken and
once again silenced, NOW it is a secret. Somehow I
can't write about secrets. My secrets, sure, because I
have authority over them. But other people's secrets
that I am keeping, not in the form of agreed upon
confidentiality, but in the form of bile tasting shame,
red hot embers of shattered assumptions and withheld
origin stories.

What I have no words for are the feelings in my heart learning of this truth. Health problems rendered a necessity for him to unearth his heredity, his genetic loading, to help doctors diagnose and accurately treat him. So with reluctance he asked for my help to get his non-identifying information. That's what they call it "non-identifying information"—yet it identified, not the name of his birth mother or his father. No they remain nameless, unidentified. But there on page three of the report, the history that caused my heart to break.

9. Poetry

'Write poems, women.' I want to
read them. I have seen you watching, holding on and
watching, and
I see your eyes moving. You have stories to tell,
strong stories; I want to hear your minds as
well as hold your hands.

—Honor Moore

Poetry is a wonderful form to express something in a new way. Its rules are different than prose. You don't have to "make sense" or sound logical. Your lines don't have to be all the same size. You can draw on memory and hearsay and first thought and emotion. You can start with a word, image, sound or a feeling, like that heaviness in the pit of your stomach which reminds you of the day you were sick in elementary school and your mother was working so your *Zaydie* (grandfather) had to pick you up. Or the pounding like thunder in your chest on a stormy winter day when the dog needs to go out out out and all you want to do is to stay inside and read read read.

The three of us got together for an afternoon at Ahava's studio on Butterstone Farm and wrote poetry. On that day she encouraged us to let our sensory responses and emotions free on the page, while attempting short line lengths and interesting word choices. We each named our poems, too!

We invite you to take a chance on poetry and let the words do their own dance. Use free association, or repeat the same vowel sounds, or try not to rhyme at all. Most of all, have fun. Poetry is about play and possibility—with words and with the journey of our lives. Enjoy!

Poetry Writing Prompt

Here's one of Ahava's poems to inspire your own poem writing:

Ars Poetica

Show up at the page
and be open to what is
happening around you.

Tell the truth as
you feel it in your bones
coursing through your heart.

Make it vivid as the sun
illuminating the cedar outside
your bedroom window.

Pull back the curtain on
another play about living this
moment as inside as it gets.

Don't stop writing.
Whatever you do.

Keep the fingers jumping
against the possibility of
blank thought.

There are always more,
don't let them get away.

Your mind is a camera
that catches the tip of ideas
as they fling against the
car window.

Drive slowly, deliberately.
There is no where to go
but here.

And you are playing
with lightning.

Let it sizzle across the
sky-like screen.

Become transparent to
yourself, willing to see
what you truly believe
about who you are and
who the world is.

Taste fear and swallow it
with a smile on your face
and a good burp.

Know it can't hurt you
but the indigestion will
free you if you wash it
down with faith.

AHAVA

I started writing poetry in my early twenties; the poems came to me as I was writing in my journals. Some inner impulse told me to play with how the words looked on the page, to experiment with sounds, images, meanings and feelings. I wasn't a poetry major, never understood the poetry we analyzed in high school. I started to connect my current thoughts with memories, or with things I had read the other week. I dropped extra words like the, and, to, for. The process was exhilarating, giving me a new way to work with the material of my life. Writing poetry helped me to explore the painful experiences I had grown up with. It also helped me retell those experiences, with new language and new meanings.

Small Red Fruit

Supple, bouncing on the
palm like a child on
the trampoline
memories of yo-yos and
super balls
things that come and go

returning to the scene
of the affair
letter A scratched into

the wooden beam above the
bed

her throat
tickled with musk
the odour of rotten
eggs, a path with
dirt, stones and tiny
footprints

her cheeks have
bruises

she waits until
the round mound
falls, green
edge earthwise
a trickle of sap

she walks barefoot
on pebbles, holds her
fingers splayed out

the gesture for
empty

her tongue squishy

she is a dreamer
the tree exhales
an unpicked life

WENDY

I never had blood sisters, which is why my closest of womenfriends have become my sisters. When I was young, my mother had a stillborn baby girl before I was born. Much later, after my mother had died, Corrie and I were clearing out things in her bedroom closet. I discovered hospital documents that described that the girl fetus stopped breathing about one week before delivery and was strangled by her umbilical cord. My mother waited one week and then delivered the dead fetus. Three years after that, I was born.

The story I remember my brother telling me when I was a young girl was different. It went like this: "A baby was born before you. She was a girl. When she was born she cried out 'Stuart, Stuart' and then she died." He later denied ever telling me this story, but I couldn't have made this up myself.

Stuart, Stuart

I was
wanted
planned
the apple
the gift
the daughter
in the right position
oh such plans
pink bedroom
ballet shoes
the whole shebang
the girl
who could have

had it all
glowingly dressed
to the little girl nines
everything taken care of
no worries
connected to the
umbilicus
nourished
and
such plans
so perfect
big brother
dentist father
doting mother
it was all
waiting for me—
and then I died.
what to do?
no cause
nothing to do
cord of nourishment
somehow wrapped
around my tiny throat
strangled by
all the plans
dance lessons
subordination
answer to dreams
now just
shuttering memories
relinquishing my life
so you could fulfill
all their dreams.

LYNDA

Mother Love

Great Mother
Tender buds
Open
    You are the living earth beneath my feet.

Ancient cedar tree
Deepening vital
Connection
    You are the living earth beneath my feet.

I call upon
Nature's wisdom
To be a "good mother" to my sons
    They are the living earth of me.

My child
You have sapphire eyes like mine
    I am the living earth of you.

I did not grow up seeing
A reflection of myself
I do not have my adoptive parents' DNA.
    I am the chosen love within their hearts.
Tickled by the Great Mother's
Dangling jade moss
From the low branch
Daydreaming, wondering if my birth mother
Regrets giving me away?
    She gave me life then fell to her knees to pray.
    She asked God, her living earth, to care for me.

At Duck Creek Park
I pause near the elbow in the stream
Wondering if my body will
Have MS like hers?
    I prayed to the living earth beneath my feet.

A water lily
In the pond
Long stem deeply rooted
Like my love for you, my child
    Mother love is the living earth beneath our feet.

Loving, giving, selfless
My other mother
Who gave me a name
And made me her own.
    She is the loving earth beneath my feet.

My mothers
You are living earth within my heart.

My sons
You are my heart
pulsing over the earth beneath my feet.

10. Dialogue Writing

*All journal writing is a result of the ongoing conversation
we are having... dialogue taps us into the greater intelligence
of our minds. We break through our defenses and confusion
to our intuitive understanding of what's going on... an exercise in learning to honor and trust our inner voices.*

—CHRISTINA BALDWIN

Using dialogue as a journal writing tool can help us
clarify and release feelings, tap into our intuition and
open to different parts of ourselves. We become both
questioner and respondent. We may access a younger
inner child voice or a critical older parent voice or a
compassionate wise woman voice or a different voice
we cannot identify or recognize. We may dialogue
with parts of our bodies, other people (alive or not;
imagined or known), objects, places, homes, feelings,
careers or jobs, animals, spirit guides, decisions, conflicts, fantasies—the possibilities are endless.

If you are new to the practice of dialogue, you may
wish to begin by having one "voice" pose a question
and then let the other "voice" respond. Once you feel
comfortable with this, you can move into a more flowing conversation, like Lynda did in her journal entry
below in which she wrote a prose dialogue between
her mother and writer voices. After you finish the dialogue, you may choose to do as Wendy did and reflect
on the insight and message you receive from it.

Step One:

**Create a list of several different aspects of your-
self: roles, jobs, emotions, personalities, likes, dis-
likes, obsessions. Use descriptive words to identify**

Journal Writing Prompt

125

those different parts, for example: Hard Worker, Shy Girl, Sassy Lady, Wise Woman.

Step Two:

Choose two aspects you feel drawn to. Write a dialogue between them. Begin your dialogue by making a statement or posing a question.

LYNDA

I am a mother who writes.

I am a mother. Baby suckling at my left breast, sure he would rather my right as it is full, large, waiting for his lips to beckon warm sweet mama juices from my flesh into his belly. But I need my right hand to write. To free-fall words, ideas, feelings, onto blank white paper.

I reach around you cradled in my arms. You breathe deeply my baby boy, snorting your way into sleep's surrender. To what am I surrendering? To you sweet child, I surrender to you and to this empty page all at once.

My identity is shifting and deepening and fraying, like the seams of this old dress I have had for years— still so bold in many colours yet the button holes are stretched bigger than the round needed to hold cloth together. What openings are too large for me right now? Which spaces are too small squeezing me out, pressing into me and urging movement to wider places?

You are so small sweet one; I feel so big, with my wings open wide, wider than that. I must be an eagle resting in the big nest outside the window, warming my eaglets, not wanting them to fall from high places. Yet they also have wings born from my feathered self. They too soar, eyes wide open, wings opening and folding in flight for life.

I will plant your afterbirth under a small tree on Mother's Day, next to the magnolia rich with soil nourished from the placenta that fed your brother. Two trees, two sons, two frozen placentas are hard evidence of your respective births. You are in my lap now, after once being beneath my skin. My heart beats for you, cell by cell, now my heart beats because of you. My hand pulses with words. I am a mother who writes. Your life gives me line upon line of myself becoming more of who I was born to be.

AHAVA

Confidence: I am here on the page where I belong, writing about this feeling of wanting to love everyone, that's my business, Love business. Not busy-ness, business as in enterprise, ongoing sustained focus and commitment to practice.

Doubt: Whatareyoutalkingabout,youhaven'tbeen here for weeks, you are a fake, a phony, a fraud.

Confidence: Well, that's exactly what keeps me from believing in myself, those thoughts. But what if nothing else mattered? What if this is all I really want to do?

Doubt: You've said that about meditating this week, and walking and being with Greg.

Confidence: I get it. I am so on the verge of something here, if I can just stay present with it. I may not have been writing, but I've been organizing, rereading, listening to

	my thoughts, writing down my goals. All parts of being a writer.
Doubt:	Unconvincing.
Confidence:	Besides I am so much more enjoying this writing than your ideas and opinions. I keep wanting to be here more.
Doubt:	You are a sexy, attractive woman, desirable, lovable.
Confidence:	I get it. I am being asked to pay attention to you, not dismiss you, and also not give you more air time than necessary.
Doubt:	You are smart, funny, give to others, friendly.
Confidence:	It's the words, my voice, my way to share my story, what I've learned, keep learning with others. It's my heart, its ways, its poisons and pathos. It's my joy, my ecstasy, the listening, echoes of who I am becoming. This is the teaching I want to do now. This I, this writer, thinker, healer.
Doubt:	I am humbled. I hear you, surrender.
Confidence:	Thanks!

WENDY

Hopeful, Successful Facilitator (HSF): I am truly jazzed about this last workshop at the retreat centre. It really jelled for me and I know it was supposed to happen.

Doubting, Vulnerable Writer (DVW): I enjoyed it too. But I know I am not truly fulfilled.

HSF: You are supposed to be more connected to and trusting of this vision than before. You are able to write. You shared your poem and *Sun* submission.

DVW: But my actual writing is not up to snuff. You may feel successful but I don't.

HSF: We shouldn't be at odds. You love to write. It's your nourishment. Yes, your words are not as eloquent as Ahava's or as insightful and piercing as Lynda's. But that's ok. You have your own way, your own voice.

DVW: I'm not one of your students. I don't need to be coddled. I am still waiting in the wings.

HSF: Do you need a plan? It seems to me you have what you've always needed, plus a supportive inspiring circle—tribe of writing goddesses. Doing the workshops will inspire you more.

DVW: I am ready for more of a challenge. Finally ready. I have visions of completion I've never felt. I need to have faith and trust. No one can give that to me.

HSF: I will try to facilitate your blossoming. Why not! It can't be that hard, can it? I want to at last trust my self. To be present in this lovely minute. To know I cannot fail. To take risks. To follow through is to honour life.

DVW: I must confront my own censors, my own harsh critics. I believe I am meant to write. To put it out for others—anyone—to see it is wholly possible. It is not egotistical or lofty. It is real and ordinary.

Insight: There is a struggle. I am unsure how to fully support my self.

Message: Stop Struggling.

11. Past, Present and Future

Look closely at the present you are constructing. It should look like the future you are dreaming.

—ALICE WALKER

Putting pen or pencil to paper connects us to the present moment, while it is also a vehicle to travel back in time or ahead into the future, depending on the point of view you choose. When we write in our journals, we are channelling different time frames, perspectives and states of mind. We can dwell on, return to or document the past, pay attention to the present and/or project, zoom and dream into the future. The past-present-future continuum is ever-present when we write.

We can never know the whole story, whether it's our past, or future or some aspect of the present that lies somewhere outside of our attention. Journal writing allows us to tune into parts of ourselves that lie on this edge. Everything may feel crazy or unmanageable in the outer world, but when we write, some internal organizing principle takes over and we start to see the larger picture.

<table>
<tr><td>**Journal Writing Prompt**</td><td>**Allow yourself to travel... write about what happened last year, last month, last week and yesterday, and what you hope will happen a week and a month from now. End with what's happening now.**</td></tr>
</table>

WENDY

Six months ago returning to Oregon, viewing the retrospective of my past lives, having lived in Portland for the past sixteen years. Spending time with our sister-friends Lana and Lyra. Exchanging massages with Krystee who I met at massage school. Teaching the lesbian writing workshop at Breitenbush. Checking out the Feminist Archives I donated to the amazing *In Other Words Bookstore and Community Center,* one of the only remaining feminist community bookstores in North America. Hanging out with the "Beach Girls," our multi-cultural, generational, sexual-preferenced amalgamation—who all met in the women's studies department at PSU—for our annual weekend at the beach.

Last month's excitement of creating a collage poem for gay pride, "Love at Second Sight," a mixture of words, images and photographs, telling the story of how Corrie and I met at the women's music festival in Yosemite. Thoroughly engaged in a new art expression, to be hung in my first art showing. The weekend so full and rich with queer consciousness and celebration. Grateful to be part of this island's queer and visible community.

Last week in Santa Cruz, returning to my past intimacies, deep friendships and long ties to sweet women friends. Rekindling the time together with Marilyn and Laura, and our leaderless radical therapy group that met for years. The one-room beach cottage Djuna dog and I retreated to after heartbreak and leaving Portland. Walking with Martha along the Santa Cruz ocean waters, shimmering sun beating down. And Nita who reminded me of the nude beach on East Cliff Drive we actually had keys to. We missed her graduation and ate magic mushrooms instead and swam in the ocean.

Yesterday in my playroom with Nora, a private journal writing workshop and sharing. Satisfying and enriching for us both, again gently reminding me of the power and depth of writing for ourselves, the necessity, the richness.

And the regrets of loss of connections with those no longer on this physical plane. Each moment we have choices. The confusion of the complexities in acknowledging the past, contemplating the future and navigating how this synthesizes into what we call present. Isn't this as well an illusion, that there is something—some plane of existence—that is only here and now?

AHAVA

Do not speak. Hold your tongue
in the centre of the fire and wait.

Touch this silence with every caw
of raven. Taste it as pulp in lemon

water, red lily on the path before
turning. Time is a mystery worth

savouring for some rainy Tuesday
or Wednesday when the limits of

words have left the bed unmade.
It is this and only this that you

will remember. Chime of sunshine
in maples, shadows on the deck.

Breathe into gravity. Empty yourself
to an open pasture. Your gates have

been released from their duty. Sit
now. Do not speak. Hold your tongue

in the centre of the fire and wait.

LYNDA

There was a time long ago, when I did not know you.
Last night we danced naked in our living room, drank
wine and listened to Neil Young as we lowered to the

floor to kiss. We once had only a brief past together—that one breakfast at Rose's in Fulford, the first night you slept over at my place on North Beach Road—you were tucked into my single bed, so was I, when the phone rang and it was my birth mother calling me for the first time, ever. You listened in the dark as I learned where I come from.

Our past is widening, our shared years growing—our family of you, me and our boys—reaching out deeper into who we are as four and as one. It is getting harder to remember a past without you in it, my sweet Pedro. It is impossible to imagine a future—a time off in the distance in which our lives could be otherwise. So I stay here, in the moment, attached to each morning coffee shared together, each kiss goodnight—I linger with the sound of you packing the boys' lunches in the morning while I bathe in the next room. I savour the beauty of your art carved in stone, etched in daily life. I love you more now than yesterday and I open to an even bigger love tomorrow and the day after that. But for now, I am here—loving you into infinity times three—in the only moment we have for sure—now.

12. Writing Goals

My journal is the seedbed for everything I write, the place where no judgment applies, not even my own... Everything I come to understand about myself is a deepening of the potential for my own writing, because it is an increase in wisdom in understanding, and in the possibility of empathy, without which no writing can ever be great.

—PAT SCHNEIDER

Sometimes we write just to write, other times we write to speak, to have voice, to think on paper, to create, to communicate, to grieve or to simply be. There is the larger goal of writing in our lives and also the goal of this particular writing. Journalling about our writing goals can propel us into greater intimacy and clarity while helping to direct our energy and focus.

Although we have found a place in our journals to explore some of our public writing goals, not everyone will have a writing goal that involves publishing and sharing their writing in the world. Some of us are content to maintain our own journal writing practices. So that's the goal: to create the journalling habit.

Journal Writing Prompt

Choose one of the following questions

• **Why do you write?**

• **At this moment, what are your writing goals?**

• **What writing projects are calling you?**

• **What I would really like to write about is.....?**

LYNDA

Immediately I think of projects, the many file folders I have on shelves, black crates, vanilla folders, books that are started, article ideas, outlines, Air Canada napkins with jotted notes, more ideas on cue cards in my little box, sketches of book covers, it's like the ingredients for a delicious batch of cookies scattered across the kitchen counter waiting to be sifted, stirred, liquid added, chocolate chips, oven on, heat, in, ten minutes, ready. Mmmmm. That's where it gets tricky. I have all the parts—the folders, ideas on top of ideas and then there is me feeling buried underneath the folders, the crates, the ideas and I am missing an egg and can't quite get it all to come together.

I feel called to focus, to pick one of these projects, including our project, and get to work. Let the words, the ideas, the motivation, presence, inspiration, purpose and the love mix together and become the intro, chapter one, chapter two, words, quotes, exercises, examples. A form takes shape, ten pages, becomes a hundred, then two-hundred and soon the pages are being glued together, a bright cover binding the pages with words and this precious soul work is held by a reader, their thinking, their actions, their self-love blossoms in relationship with the words offered on the page. This work, my work, my writing becomes a catalyst for something meaningful, transformative and vital.

WENDY

Never enough time. Never enough focus. Never as compelling as having bodies and hearts and minds in front of me. The magic of the moment. And yet books are my nourishment, my inspiration.

My hand is tingling. My writing hand. The hand that connects me to my thoughts, my vision, my inspiration. How do I take years and years of concerns and prioritizing other people's writings and turn that energy toward myself?

My goal is to document experience. To move and change and impress—as in making an impression. To confront silence. To put many things into the light. To be honest and bold and to feel courageous and determined enough to sustain engagement in this project. The power of the personal, the private, the first person. To negate shame and guilt and fear. The terrible and the mundane. Privilege and oppression. How it all operates within the same person, in the varied events and textures of lives.

My fascination with writing, my obsession with writing it down. This has to mean something. I will never give it up. With Audre Lorde, Marge Piercy, Susan Griffin, Deena Metzger, Starhawk as my models. With the intensity and resilience of so many people.

It is about bringing our selves and our hearts out into the open. To say to ourselves, to each other—"Yes, I see. I feel. I know. We are in this together." It is magic.

AHAVA

During the more than twenty-seven years that I have been writing in a journal, I have had many different writing goals. When I wanted to share my poems with others, I started to write them on beautiful handmade paper and give them away to friends. Then I sought out venues where I could perform them and started speaking them aloud at readings and events where the themes of my poems were relevant and could inspire others like at conferences, festivals and in high school and university classrooms. When I wanted to publish a book, it was a much more complicated goal, as I had to gather all my poems, edit them and decide whether I would send them out or produce it myself. After choosing to self-publish, I had to settle on a title, enlist friends to do the graphic design and photography, and find a printer who would make the copies look professional.

Some of my writing goals have only manifested after years of patiently waiting for the time when I was able to focus and get the support I needed. That was why I chose to go back to school at thirty six. I wanted to focus on my writing and I found mentors who could encourage and challenge me.

The creation of this book with Wendy and Lynda has represented a goal I have long had to write a book about my passion for journal writing. Seven years is a long time to wait and work and trust. Actually, trust is a big part of writing goals. Even if the goal is to write for five or ten minutes, I still have to trust that I can find the words to fill the page for that time.

Another exciting goal I have realized is using my writing to support others. I love being a writing mentor, sharing my joy and experience with words to support others' spiritual growth and creative emergence.

I still have many more goals for my writing, including a new book of poetry, stories to be told to audiences through this voice and body, as well as a book about Loving Inquiry and the journey toward authentic self-expression.

13. Our Writing Lives

Writing is a way, and not necessarily the only way, to open up the word and the world, and our lives within that world for attention, discussion, understanding, re-imagining and re-creating, as well as for a profound acceptance of what is.

—CYNTHIA CHAMBERS

When you're driven to write, the writing is writing you, and it's like being taken—you are not where you were before or where you will be once you close your notebook.

—PATRICE VECCHIONE

If you write in some small or large way, you have a writing life. The following journal entries were created flowing from a conversation we were having about our writing lives and the dreams we each have for our writing. As we acknowledged and wrote about the power of journal writing in our lives, we realized there was a yearning to create something new, to move our writing into the world beyond the journal. What a beautiful contradiction—celebrating our journal writing, and the safety and the power of this private space of writing, and being inspired to name our visions, our dreams to share our writing out in the world.

Journal Writing Prompt **Start with "My writing life is…"**

WENDY

My writing life is brimming with ideas, fertile with phrases, inspirations and opportunities.

Facilitating the workshop—the circle of seven women writing—last weekend was PERFECT, just so perfect, as it should have been, the answer to my most vital intention. Bringing my books (from my playroom to the yurt), photocopied handouts, coloured pencils and coloured pens, candle, basket of writing trinkets (tarot decks, SARK cards, goddess images) and all the exercises, prompts, principles, approaches I know and have so graciously borrowed from wise wordswomen. Meditation chairs supporting our circle on the green rug. A meal I prepared for them in the afternoon.

At first I felt some trepidation, wondering about their response, their states of mind, assuring them (and reassuring them) of their privacy and choice in sharing (or not sharing). Allowing them the safety to truly write for themselves, among one another. And gradually a momentum all of its own began to erupt as we moved from one writing and sharing to the next. A flow, an energy, the dynamic that never fails to impress me, alerts me to the possibilities and potentials unearthed as we move ever so gently towards ourselves, our centres, the truths and richness of our lives. Such joy to behold!

LYNDA

Blocking "writing days," "writing hours" and of course this much loved "writing group" into my daily life. I am opening space in my mind to write even when my pen is not on the paper: writing as I watch Jackson zoom his Lightning McQueen car over my toes, writing as I change diapers, run shallow baths, stir powdered oatmeal to become Jesse's breakfast. I am writing before conference calls with clients and jotting notes after. I am breathing writing alongside my daily walks, letting words rise up in me as my feet hit the pavement—left foot, right foot. I am stepping into my writing like stepping into a warm, steamy bath on a cold day. I am speaking out loud some of the challenges of this "writing life" and seeking support from others especially both of you.

I feel called to writing like never before, past the privacy and companionship of my journal. I feel called to creating a relationship with readers, beyond this loving relationship with myself on the page. I am making space for my adoption memoir project *Umbilical Cord*, moving other temptations and distractions from this path of longing and just Friday, waiting in the rain for a tow truck to lift our Air Stream trailer with a blown-out tire onto the flatbed truck, I created a mind map, a project plan with timelines and structure for my writing. Yes, writing, not thinking about writing, or planning for writing, or dreaming of writing, or reading about writing, or signing up for another writing workshop or retreat, but the actual WRITING itself starts with earnest and passion and trepidation and deep presence this week. Thursday to be exact, from 10-3 at my studio—my place of purple and yellow and all-chakra energy, books, floor mats, paper, pens, and my window seat cushioning years of journals beneath it in the cedar box—holding me and my life, ready to crack it wide open into the heart of my memoir, into the heart of myself and my becoming so far.

AHAVA

My writing life is, wow, opening up so full just like the potential of this house I now sit in. The walls will soon come down, the windows will shift positions, a new roof put on to make it into something else, a space for me to be at home in, to nurture myself. Just like I do in my writing life which I said is now about to expand out to who knows where as I take a chance by allowing others to guide and support me toward sharing my poems and voice in the world. Into the production, design, editing. The foundation is set, the colours will brighten, the lines sharpen, the shape of the work will come into focus. I thought it would happen again but didn't know when. Here it is! The two meetings I am set to have in the next two days will make it possible for me to move into the next phase of writing again, performance and publishing. How it will look I don't know but that it will happen I know for sure.

My writing life is growing in other ways too through the PhD and new poems to be birthed out of me. It is exciting to be working with the material I have written since coming to Salt Spring, to give that body of work an audience beyond here, to give the poems away. And meditation, the farm, are containers to hold me, support me and Gregory, my best friend on this journey of evolving my writing life.

Like the trees here on the farm, so diverse and bountiful, so may my writing be, so may I no longer hoard the poems but let them drop like apples. Some may bruise and become compost, others will be picked and placed in someone else's hands to be enjoyed, nurturing and satisfying and nourishing their heart. That is the path of my writing life as it is now unfolding. Wow. And I thought I was writing just for me. And have been. But always the desire, secret and loud inside, to share, to read aloud, to offer poems and other words as sustenance. With help. I am asking and able to receive help now from others.

14. Relating To The Term Writer

I want my words to serve as women's art has always served—white stitched quilts, sienna pots, woven water wheels, spears, bows, houses. To carry food, keep warm, pass on the muscle of those who stood and those who fell. Words to be a place to come home to.

—ELLEN BASS

All my life my writing has led me beyond what I thought I knew...I have always written out of the experience of my own life, beginning with acutely personal feelings. For this I believe is the paradox of art. In the very specific, one discovers a universal design; in the familiar terrain of one's own soul, one finds the answers to mysteries.

—SUSAN GRIFFIN

Are we writers or do we write? Does identifying as a writer empower us or does it create pressures that stifle or even silence us? Do we create obstacles by questioning our identities as "real" (serious) writers? What is the tension between labelling what we do as "journal writing" versus "writing"?

We have learned the importance of focusing on the process, rather than the product, to give ourselves the confidence we desire in order to write freely. Journal writing is its own genre, as real and rich, standing proud alongside any form of writing.

It is our writing that propels us into the writing sphere. Being engaged with our writing, in whatever context, validates and supports our continuing to write. Writing together within our circles provides this constancy in our writing practice and encourages us to identify ourselves as women who write by writing.

Wendy Writes...

We enter into the craft of writing by writing.

Ahava Writes...

I am a writer. I have a voice for the world.

Lynda Writes...

When I don't get to my writing, something in me changes.

How do you relate to the term "writer"? What would it mean to write on your own terms?

Journal Writing Prompt

Experiment and discover what works best for you. How can you bring this sense of experimentation and play into your own writing practice?

WENDY

To discover—who I was, who I am, who I can be

To figure out the SIGNIFICANT EVENTS, TURNING POINTS, OBSTACLES, INSIGHTS

How I struggled to BECOME the person I am (sounds so ego-focused and un-buddhist)

INFLUENCES—major influences on my life and consciousness

IMPORTANT FEMINIST HERSTORY—what was going on around and about me

THE HERSTORY OF MY CONSCIOUSNESS-RAISING

MEMOIR—The Story of Me (and how so important I am!)

COMING OUT—coming to myself, my centre, my authenticity

IMPETUS TO DOCUMENT—this has been an intention all along

To record, acknowledge, validate, put down, eschewing the censors and honouring truth

TOWARDS CHANGE AND EVOLUTION—the potential wisdom that comes from this

For me? For the "world?" For others?

Putting these principles into practice

TOWARDS PUBLICATION—combined memoir and journal-writing handbook

JOURNAL WRITING PROJECT—gathering stories,

share, collaborate on

THE TRUTH OF OUR LIVES—brutal and joyful

QUESTIONING, COMPLEXITIES, TRUTH, THE PRESENT MOMENT,

FEAR, VULNERABILITY, TRUSTING, LEARNING, FREEDOM,

SELF-NOURISHMENT, SELF-AWARENESS, SELF-VALIDATION, SELF-ACCEPTANCE,

A DEEPLY FELT LIFE

AHAVA

Does it matter I relate to it, or that I just be it because if I think about it I am probably going to say I'm not really a writer because I don't have so many books on the shelves. But if I breathe into it, or simply watch these hands as they dance on the page like this, then who cares how I relate? I have been relating on the page for so long, it is where I find my soul my body my heart. Yes, I have the heart of a writer, the soul of a writer. I have been writing for so long I don't even wonder what I am going to say when I start on the page, don't think whether it will make sense. Whose sense am I making? I don't really care if anyone reads this. I read it though. I stumble into writing with the heart of a hungry wolf and the joy of a two- year-old twirling in the grass.

Who sets the terms for writer? Who says what it means? How many books are we supposed to have published, how many poems have to be printed in literary journals?

This week I have sent out a new poem, barely dry, to hundreds of people through email and I received such lovely feedback. The vulnerability, wondering if they would like my poem. If they would like me.

But the poem itself, its languaging and its gorgeous interpretation of what it means for me to be human, to be among birds and learn impermanence and freedom, that is how I relate, how I term myself. The writer who expresses her being through words, who finds meaning and refuge in a page of scribbles about birds, light and partners, hurts and unknown futures.

Writer is a term of endearment. This writer is a being impressed by cold, heat, wind, rain and waters flowing over stones in creeks and toppling down mountains after knee-high snowfalls. This writer relates to the world through words. Those are her terms for writing, the vulnerability, any emotion felt, the connections with friends, or family or lack thereof. Is there anything this writer would not want to write about? She often writes about fires and creative sparks and this morning it was her body's stories unfurled from moving limbs.

How gorgeous is that?! The studio dreamed into and realized, a creative oasis in a quiet room. How she loves to be there with words, loves to be anywhere with words. This writer smiles wide, and snatches of poems are birthed. How many layers of files, how many degrees of separation crossed through the words on the page in years of unknown and self-cared-for terms?

These are her terms: write into this life, about this life, for the refuge, healing, nourishment, joy and sweet miracles of stories created and characters integrated and landscapes make-believed and peace conceived. Oh the glorious emergence of possibilities, of worlds out of pen tips and mind flips on a switch and there it is, imagination, opening to play. Let's start again… This is how I create the terms for who I am as a writer. This is the beauty of it, how I write, when, where, for whom and why and why not? Now we're getting into my terms. Writing on our own terms, that's it. What are the terms you want to name, reframe so you can fully claim your writing?

LYND A

I am a writer. I like the sound of this. They (whoever "they" are) say that what we envy in others is something we desire for ourselves. I envy authors. Anytime I am at a book reading, a book launch—as I watch the author read an excerpt from her book, I think to myself "I wish that was me."

I relate to the term writer with deep desire. Then I have to remind myself, I already am a writer—this thing I long for already exists (as is often the case in life). To be clear then, I want to be a published author—with many books to my credit—not for myself only, but to know these books went out and touched lives the way so many books and authors have touched my life.

I relate to the term writer wholeheartedly, it feels like an identity and a calling that resides in my DNA, although I can't be sure of that, given I am adopted and know only half, or less, of my biological history.

Or maybe I was a writer in a past life. Perhaps I was also a graphic designer, as I could look at business logos all day—and maybe an exotic dancer, as I love to be naked and dance. I digress. That's what journal writing lets me do: digress, decide and dream what I want to. I can make a point, craft a path and then I can take a detour—go someplace else—on the page or in my life. I have captured a lot of twists and turns—subtle and not so subtle—the many dips and dives of living—have been witnessed and designed through writing. I relate to the term writer, the way I relate to life—wholeheartedly, most of the time.

15. Rereading Our Journals

The writing outlasts jobs, partners, and pets. The writing itself is the continuum of our lives.

—LARAINE HERRING

What rock must we turn over to uncover the details of our story?

—FERRON

Rereading our journals can be as simple as: Going over the last few words we have written to see what triggered our train of thought, glancing at a paragraph in an entry from a few days or weeks ago or pulling out our past journals to revisit what we were going through at a specific point in our lives.

When rereading our journals, we have the opportunity to witness our own growth and evolution as well as to recognize the places where we get stuck. It puts us in touch with our personal resilience and provides us with concrete evidence of our experience.

It takes courage to write about the challenges of our lives. We require just as much courage to go back and read about them again. We can make the rereading safe and meaningful by coming back to the page with an attitude of self-acceptance and curiosity. Even over the course of a few minutes, and especially after many years, we change—physically, emotionally, mentally, our thoughts and feelings shift, our needs, desires and habits differ. Sharing the process of rereading our journals with others in the circle is an intimate and inspiring experience.

147

Journal Writing Prompt **What is your experience with rereading your journals?**

If you do not have any journals to reread or if you have destroyed or lost them, you can find old letters, notes, photographs or scrapbooks to look at and reread.

LYNDA

I visit you like a friend I have not seen in years, yet know intimately. I am passing backwards in time, backwards in my own lived experience, as if meeting some of my own life for the first time. I read passages of pain, epiphany, decision and I can barely remember certain moments even though they were mine, all mine. I reread pages and they are not blank sheets of papers with words, but rather memories, years, minutes and seconds of my life. I find exquisite descriptions of lovers—details such as where he placed his hand, or how I walked away, pages of when I laid down, when I waited, when I wanted. I turn the page and a week has passed and there the page is filled with the hours leading to my grandmother's death, turn one page to my mother's mastectomy the next day January 13, 1997, January 14, 1997. I reach into the Rubbermaid container and pull out another spiral bound sketch book filled with words and I am at a coffee shop along the Champs Elyseés in Paris, my backpack at my feet, my Swiss friend reading across from me. We just finished reminiscing about our adventure the night before along the Moulin Rouge, I was twenty maybe twenty-one.

I cry as I reread my journals—tears for what I remember and what I forget. Would my own life have the same depth and breadth without these pages filled with words? Would I have the same depth?

Dear Journal, you are a guide. As I read back into you, I touch profound places within myself—corners that lack exit, wide open spaces with so much yet to explore, small dark crevices, fields of wild flowers so sweet, you are an angel, a landmark, a mystery, I can see into myself as I reread you. I see my own becoming on your pages—in black, blue, red, purple, green, indigo—the pages of coloured ink, the chakras embodied on white—no lines. I reread only one journal with lines. I look back to blank pages, filled, roamed upon, footprints of my soul marked by fast moving pen on paper. You are me, I am you.

WENDY

1977. I grabbed for what I call my "favourite" journal, covered in blue-and-white velvet stars. Sally made it when working part-time for Emily, who sold journals on the "Ave" (Telegraph Avenue in Berkeley). Forcing me to process this time of tumult, exploration, rejection, romance, revolving emotions.

Coming out is never one motion but a mixture of incidents, desires, fears, vulnerabilities, interacting and interchanging over years. It began in 1974, January 1st to be exact, that first night Sandra and I slept together in her upstairs bedroom, the night before our other three housemates returned from xmas break. By 1977, as my relationship deepened with Sally, and we began living together, the conflicts arose to a monumental level.

I was at last experiencing the joy of engagement in a serious love and passionate relationship with a woman. I was attempting to come to terms with my place in the university and the graduate program I was enrolled in. I was comprehending my deepening politics and my commitment as well as the responsibility this assumed. I was preparing to visit China as part of a delegation. Surprised to find some of the strongest memories in my experiences dealing with my parents' rejection of my loving a woman and living my life as a lesbian.

AHAVA

Sometimes I am going about my daily life and an event that happened years ago resurfaces, tugs at me to be revisited more fully. When I finally find the right journal, I am often amazed at the discrepancy between what I thought would be contained there and what is actually written. Strange as it seems, I often remember different details than what I chose to write about.

One of the most important lessons I have learned from my experiences of rereading has been how vital it is for me to return to my journal pages with a feeling of humility, compassion and kindness toward the self I was when I was writing those pages. I have to recognize the "me" who is now reading these pages is not the same "me" who was writing them.

As I read again, I excavate, explore, understand, uncover truth, or truths, watch the miracle of my growing selves, my being in its process of becoming, notice how I learn, what I focus on, what I choose to write about and what not. Self-study.

I am curious about my own learning and how I teach myself to love, to be present, to cope, to keep on when I too, like John Mayer, want to "stop this train and get off."

I am interested in the way I tell my life, the discourses I use, the influences, what assumptions I am living by. I am curious about my own freedom. What does freedom mean? I think I mean freedom from suffering, like the Buddha talks about. Freedom from dangerous mind, from self-judgment, from inner harm. Freedom that I gain through journal writing to practice being awake, choosing compassion, love.

Part Six:

Into the Open

We uncover our
unique strengths and gifts
and discover how we want
to share them
with the world.

—Ahava

The Heart of Transformation

If you write as a woman, you know this as I do: you write to give the body its Book of Future because Love dictates your new geneses to you. Not to fill in the abyss, but to love yourself right to the bottom of your abysses. To know, not to avoid... Not to surmount; to explore, dive down, visit.

—HÉLÈNE CIXOUS

As we share our different human experiences, we rediscover a sense of unity. We remember we are part of a greater whole. And as an added joy, we also discover our collective wisdom. We suddenly see how wise we can be together.

—MARGARET WHEATLEY

Writing Alone Together creates a sacred space for the soulful act of self-expression. Sharing our stories helps us make sense of our experiences and ignites our creativity. Providing a place to be witnessed and accepted in the truth of who we are, journalling with others opens us into compassion and empathy and brings us into connection through the healing power of words.

Writing in our most open, vulnerable and authentic ways, as we do in our journals, is an empowering and transformational process. The act of writing our feelings and thoughts on paper allows us to acknowledge and integrate them into our lives. We access greater self-awareness and free ourselves from past experiences or limiting beliefs.

Journalling is one of the most powerful ways to explore our desires and our sense of purpose. Writing about our goals and dreams and speaking them aloud helps us to manifest them more easily. A powerful alchemy emerges when we allow ourselves to be seen and heard by others.

Writing Alone Together is a process of personal learning, spiritual growth and connection with others. When we come together with the intention of being fully present, listening and sharing our words, thoughts, views, wounds, desires and visions, we create supportive and responsive communities while fostering wholeness and well-being within.

You don't have to consider yourself spiritual, or have any particular beliefs, to benefit from these practices. Simply connect with your breath, feel your aliveness, pick up your pen and begin.

Wendy Writes...

To write for oneself is to reach for deeper clarity and understanding. It is an act of reverence. I fully believe that the more in touch we each are with our own lives, struggles, joys, challenges, desires, the better in tune we are to imagine the changes and the world we want to create. We need opportunities, rituals in our lives to defuse the pain, the speed, the distractions of modern life and to calm and nourish ourselves. Journal writing is a rich resource for self nourishment and healing. It is something that will never abandon us, as long as we have access to pen, pencil and paper or laptop. Journal writing is accessible to all and can be used towards our most personal, political and world-transforming goals.

Writing Alone Together transforms our experience of ourselves as writers. Our writing improves through this opportunity to journal, read and listen to one another's writing. Instead of critique, we embark on a different way of learning how to write. The four practices sharpen our craft and content as writers. Our writing expands as we explore the diversity of our voices and are encouraged to express ourselves freely and in new ways. We feel more empowered to write, dream about writing, call ourselves "writers" and take the steps to share our writing in the world, if we choose to do so.

I have found in my self... an authentic desire for a wider communion, a sharing of meaning, a connectedness.

—Susan Griffin

We are living amidst tremendous social, political and spiritual change. We are called to create a stronger sense of community with one another and the planet. We need ways of coming together to collaborate and infuse our lives with a spirit of connection in order to heal, grow and evolve. Writing Alone Together brings women into nourishing, creative relationships with one another, our communities and the world, while supporting us to deliver our voices and wisdom into the spiral of awakening that is rising in our midst.

Our Final Journal Entries: Journalling about Transformation

A circle is a way of doing things differently than we have become accustomed to. The circle is a return to our original form of community, as well as a leap forward to create a new form of community.

—Christina Baldwin

How have I been transformed through the act of Writing Alone Together?

Journal Writing Prompt

We responded to this prompt in separate locations and brought our writing together to share.

WENDY

Writing *Writing Alone Together* has been challenging, stimulating, tedious, engaging, interminable, joyful, exhausting, inspiring and completely captivating and transformative.

Here I write (print) on this journal covered by a brown goddess holding a white dove with a rainbow heart on her chest. Another journal, another entry, another writing alone together alongside my writing sisters, goddesses, lovelies. Here I am. Here we are. Here I write.

This book you are now reading has taken its own time to birth. Our collaboration has been life changing, forcing us to question our motives, challenge our views, listen more carefully and reaffirm our commitment to this book and to one another. This co-creation has been a way for me to merge my love for collaboration, journal writing and intimacy with women.

Witnessing vast changes in political, social, cultural and personal landscapes, my journal provided me a safe place to process, record and question. Journal writing saved my life because without it I would be adrift. Journal writing is not an insignificant or trivial act. The practice of writing my life has transformed me. And I have, in turn, transformed my world.

During walks in the forest, along the ocean, accompanied by my dog companions, I was never without a journal. Long ago, I wrote in my journal, "I write because I need to write. I write because I want to, perhaps in another life, perhaps always. I feel this putting down words is familiar and very, very old and yet feels always new."

Writing is what I do. It frees and focuses me at the same time. I like to watch the lines of the letters as my pen creates these forms. I never know where I will journey. There is no particular destination. It is a way: to keep going, transformation-in-the-making; to honour those who have come before; to mourn the loss of loved ones, lovers, dying friendships, movements and organizations; to rage against injustice, inequity and the ravages of oppression in all its varying forms; to document herstory and uncover the truths of our ordinary and extraordinary lives; and to be engaged in this process of radical change and transformation which is the essence of life.

My passion is to inspire others, particularly women, to honour the power and truth of their lives. Writing Sisters. I choose my sisters—the women in my life who love me, share with me, honour me by their presence. Their presence is truly a present, their gift to me.

I am nourished by these fertile circles of women. I am moved by witnessing their courage, resilience, beauty. Discovering my own strength through recognizing their fortitude, their flowing feelings, even their pain. I am guided by their infinite and varied wisdom as we gather, alone and together.

These practices keep me sane, in touch and transcendent all at the same time. Through transitions, changes, moves, disruptions, illnesses, losses, even deaths, journal writing is the life line to my ever-deepening heart, witnessing it all. My intense wish is for our beloved *Writing Alone Together* to be a refuge, a spark, an inspiration into this journey of writing among others.

And now, as I reflect upon the vast array of books I have filled with the connections, chaos and churning of my life, I know, in the way you know something deeply, securely, fervently, that I will be continuing to do this until I take my last breath.

AHAVA

It happens, sometimes without our knowing it: we live into the next phase of our life. Of course, we may have been dreaming about it for a long time. If I look back at my journals I can see there was a thread I was following. I can actually follow it back to the very beginning, that very first journal. Or maybe it was in the third or fourth that I started to locate an intention to share my journey in this way, with words, and with attention to stories and feelings, thoughts and their origins in culture, gender, family.

Today, nearly twenty-five years later, I sit here at the local authentic Italian pizza place on Salt Spring and feast on a single slice of Sicilian vegetarian loaded with artichokes, red peppers, tomato sauce, onions and cheese. Every mouthful is ridiculously delicious, a festive gathering of flavours on my tongue. Much like the gathering we three are celebrating in our book *Writing Alone Together*.

I want to take another bite but I have said I wouldn't eat the last quarter until I finish this writing. What is it about writing that both pulls me down to it and pushes me away? Truth, in both instances, as in this pizza tastes so good whereas the sharing of vulnerability sometimes hurts. However there is relief in the admitting of feelings or an experience I had been hiding within me.

There is no hiding here on the page when it releases from me like this. We call it free writing. And where is the transformation? Could I leave that topic for another day? The topic as we have said is always a suggestion. These are mostly raw words, and where they lead us we most often don't know—a piece of pizza, a reference to an old journal or two and the impulse to say no to another bite and yes to the pouring out of words.

It takes time to write a book, to build trust, to figure out how an impulse to share a journey with others becomes real. The pizza was once just dough and tomatoes growing on vines in someone's greenhouse. These words I know not where they come from. Certainly the same place as all the rest. My heart, the Letter Tree? It doesn't matter, as Ursula LeGuin says in *Wave of the Mind*. When we put it all together it becomes something new entirely.

Without the sun, the warm weather and the hands that held the seeds and then the seedlings, the hose, the ripe vegetables and the knife to cut them up, this writing would not be. I might have chosen another local restaurant, could have been talking about raw fish or a portabello mushroom burger.

But here I am, writing about transformation, whether of food or love or the experience of creation, the allowing of something beautiful to emerge over a period of time.

What is the right temperature for cheese to melt? What are the right conditions for three women to commit and keep committing to their writing? Amidst the doubt and fear and forgetting how lucky we are to be alive, when the process was stuck or stodgy, when we thought one of us was holding up the show because of lack of experience or ineffective communication. No naming of names. All the blame let go. What matters is the drive to keep moving past the judgment and anger and frustration. The willingness to see each other for who we are: a Goddess, a woman, a sister, a writer wanting the same dream, holding onto the same goals, dealing with the same worries and furies in different forms.

The pizza is getting cold. Only six more minutes before I have to leave. Still, time is elastic. Look how much savoury life we have shared in our entries, written five to ten minutes at a time.

LYNDA

When we started coming together to journal in our circle of three, Jesse was a newborn baby and Jackson was learning his first words and getting more capable taking steps in the world. Now, my sons are seven and a half and nine years old respectively. As I reread my writing in the pages of this book, I am struck by how so many of my own journal entries speak of things from so long ago.

Life is always changing. Transformation—or the state of being transformed—is happening every minute of every day. Many mornings I take a picture of the sunrise and post the image on Facebook, a visual timeline on my timeline. No two images are ever the same, yet I step out on our deck in the morning, stand in roughly the same location and take the picture. Snapshots are a lot like life, fleeting, ever changing.

The cells of our bodies are like this too. I once heard Deepak Chopra speak at a conference and he described the rate at which each organ of our body is completely replenished, made completely new over and over again in days, weeks, months and years—our skin, heart, pancreas, bladder, hair, all of it, all of us, completely renewed. This is why healing is possible, why wounds heal, only sometimes leaving a scar on our body, in our hearts.

Motherhood has taught me a new understanding of transformation. Last night, when I tucked Jesse into bed, I whispered in his ear, as I do each night, "Always know how much your Mommy loves you." He replied, "I do know that Mommy, because you always tell me."

Maybe this is how time is held onto, even while it is passing, through the routines and repetitive things we say and do. We etch the feelings and memories into our beings, even though they will pass and often be forgotten. Journalling is a way of remembering.

I might have forgotten about that morning years ago when I tried to go to the aqua fit class and had to get out of the water only minutes after arriving to nurse Jesse. He was only a few weeks old. I might not have remembered how I felt the day of Sue's funeral. But here it is, all written down—all this living, breathing, feeling and loving. I notice all these moments while writing and all these moments are written down. Captured like snapshots.

This morning I wrote the sound of Jackson playing his guitar, the smell of the chocolate chip cookies that just came out of the oven and the touch of my husband's hands rubbing my back, night after night. Yesterday, I wrote about frogs and how I read they are the bearers of luck and fortune, their healing powers apparently cleanse and replenish the soul.

Last week, I wrote about the amazing hike we took to the top of Reginald Hill, the wind blowing cold, my hands touching the smooth limb of the bark shedding Arbutus trees. Nature transforming. All of us are transforming, alone and together, constantly. When we write things down, we give our desires voice, we put our experiences and intentions on the page—by doing

so, we are already engaging in a process of transformation.

Writing Alone Together in the World

"It goes on one at a time,
it starts when you care
to act, it starts when you do
it again after they said No,
it starts when you say We
and know who you mean, and each
day you mean one more."

—MARGE PIERCY

I have been part of a circle...it is one of the most import-
ant connections of my life.

—ALICE WALKER

We offer the world our lived experiences. These are our
treasures, our gifts.

—LORRAINE GANE

Here are some examples of how we weave our Writing
Alone Together practice into our respective work to
serve and benefit others.

AHAVA

One of the meaningful and exciting ways I bring the
four practices of Writing Alone Together into my work
is as a writing mentor for the intergenerational writers'
group at the local high school, organized by the Connecting Generations Program. Meeting regularly after

school, students from grades 9–12 and adults from the Salt Spring community gather around big tables to share our passion for writing.

Week after week, the writers boldly and courageously explore their voices on many topics: home, nature, family, cultural legacies, relationships, memories, dreams, joys, fears and many other human preoccupations.

Each week, I invite them to start from a prompt, whether a quote, poem, story, "word of the day," world event or other provocation. These prompts have been inspired by comments one of the writers has made in their initial check-in, music playing in another writer's ipod or a newspaper article I'd read before coming to the group. We never know where the inspiration will lead us. After our first timed writing, we listen with curiosity to the journey each has taken on the page, amazed and intrigued by the different ways we each respond to the prompt.

Making the commitment to a regularly scheduled meeting is as important to the group process as the encouragement of diversity in written expression. The mixed generations also support the writers to reach past their personal experience and discover how the world looks and feels to someone of another age and perspective.

Apart from our celebrated wordsmithing each week, we also have insightful group conversations. One week we talked about how to hold a space for every piece of writing to be seen as sacred. This was sparked by the realization that we often judge and condemn our writing before we share it with others. We noticed that sometimes, before we share a piece of writing, we say things out loud like "this isn't very good," or "I'm not sure I did the prompt correctly." In discussing why we do this, we thought it might be because we are afraid to be boastful and arrogant or we are afraid of rejection so we reject ourselves first. Paradoxically, we acknowledged how, secretly, we love the writing we do because it is ours. Our playing with words opens, inspires and nourishes us.

Another conversation centered on how girls at school are often expected and encouraged to be perfect, smart and responsible for most of the work, while the teachers say "boys will be boys" and let them get away with slacking. In response, the writers recognized how important it is for girls to find a place of confidence and affirmation inside themselves, as opposed to looking for external affirmation from teachers.

Some of the writers from the group have accompanied me in giving workshops to a whole classroom at the high school. During a one hour session, we explain the four practices and invite the students onto the page. Afterward, the students read their new writing in pairs. In the larger circle, students share their surprise at what came out and how much they enjoy being heard and hearing each others' spontaneous words.

No matter our ages, gender or skill levels, all of us enjoy being a part of this open, non-judgmental exchange, delight in this unique opportunity to connect and revel in the power and possibilities of our individual and collective imaginations.

LYNDA

I am infusing the Writing Alone Together practices in a variety of ways within my work. For example, in a recent Writing for Wellness Coaching Circle, an online group coaching program, I had three women participating from Canada, South Africa and Australia respectively. Each week, we came together for a group call and I guided them in the process of Writing Alone Together applied to various weekly themes such as self-care, gaining clarity, stress release and inner peace. Each week, I also taught journalling for health and expressive writing techniques such as affirmative writing, transactional writing, poetic writing and many more. They each loved the experience, sharing that they felt enriched, grounded, heard, expanded and nourished by this creative and collective process.

Powerful connections were made through this shared experience. In fact as I write this, Thea, the woman from Botswana, is here on Salt Spring Island for a month long solo writing retreat. She is staying at one of our cottages located across the road from our home. Last week, we got together in person with the woman from Victoria and another woman, to once again engage in Writing Alone Together. I am often in awe at the capacity writing and sharing and listening and caring can have on enriching relationships, bringing us into the heart and truth of who we are—alone and together.

I also integrate Writing Alone Together into journalling for self-care and wellness workshops that I regularly offer to helping and healthcare professionals. As helpers and healers gather together, to heal, replenish and grow, Writing Alone Together offers them a practice for engaging narrative, stories and experiences for the purposes of learning, connecting and replenishing together. These are critical factors for preventing burnout and reducing the risk for vicarious trauma and compassion fatigue, common occupational hazards within high touch fields and trauma informed work. I specialize in burnout prevention for helping professionals and for many years that was the focus of my work. However, now I focus on therapeutic writing as the vehicle for engaging the learning in this area versus more content driven teaching. Through writing, the learning is process driven offering people more time to reflect and access their own wisdom about how to balance self-care with other-care in order to make the difference they are here to make.

I am also bringing Writing Alone Together into work I do through my other business, Thrive Training and Coaching where I work with leaders, teams and organizations in the areas of change management, resiliency, employee wellness, stress management and work-life balance. Again, Writing Alone Together offers the foundation and process for bringing people together to engage in conversations about things that really matter, in ways that are respectful and compassionate. This process fosters team building, engagement, positive collegial relationships and deepens the learning by drawing upon the wisdom and lived experiences of participants in the workshop in a creative and expressive way through writing, storytelling and conversation based learning.

Next year, I am offering a new program called Open Hearted Leadership through Hollyhock, a popular retreat and learning centre located on Cortes Island, BC. Leaders will gather to explore the meaning and benefits of Open Hearted Leadership and one of the tools I will use to engage the wisdom of the group and teach emotional intelligence, a transformational leadership competency, will include the Writing Alone Together process.

Ultimately, I am using Writing Alone Together (plus other mindfulness practices and coaching tools) to foster self-awareness in myself and others, for the purpose of deepening strong reflective, relational, wellness and leadership skills to help cultivate healing, growth and transformation at the individual, team, organizational and community levels.

WENDY

It is late April with characteristic grey skies and a chilly wind. Hail pelts the ceiling above us. A circle of eighteen women fill the back of the bookstore. A gathering of women drawn to write alone together for a workshop and to celebrate the completion of *Writing Alone Together* with a (pre) book launch. I am heartened to find many old friends, past students and colleagues in this circle, as well as those I've mentored as teaching assistants, women from past writing workshops, massage clients, an eighty-two-year-old from one of the first workshops I gave, my close friend's mother from out-of-town and my thirty-four-year-old niece as well as volunteers from the bookstore and a few others.

Bringing women to write together is my work in the world. Since beginning to teach many decades ago, I have viewed myself as a "radical teacher," inspiring feminist activism and social change. As a women's studies instructor at Portland State University, where I taught for many years, I forged a community partnership with the local feminist bookstore, In Other

Words, a non-profit, volunteer-run, feminist community centre. Women's bookstores have traditionally offered more than just books, providing much-needed resources and connections with other women, support groups, meeting spaces and the richness of feminist publications, information, issues, events, controversies and so much more.

My students and I helped organize author readings, benefits for feminist organizations and other events such as speakers' panels, film showings and discussions. Many classes culminated in readings of students' creative projects. Much of these stemmed from the journal writing we engaged in and the reading, listening, sharing and witnessing.

I now use what we call the Writing Alone Together Practices, Principles and Prompts convening women's writing circles. As women become used to writing and sharing their writing with one another, they also feel encouraged to bring their own ideas for creative projects and collaborations into practice. Twice a year, I organize solstice gatherings of women who are in the circles I facilitate to meet together in a larger circle of women writing together. We each bring our stories and lives into the circle, reading aloud and listening deeply. This turns into a profound sharing that affirms each of us as writers and, more than that, as part of a shared community.

The work I continue to do in the world, the passion I bring to teaching, facilitating workshops and guiding circles of women, inspires women to find their own voices, stories, perspectives and a sense of connection and collaboration with others that is so vital in these times of alienation, aloneness and separation that so many of us experience. Writing Alone Together becomes a lifeline, a nourishing and revitalizing infusion of creativity, compassion and connection.

In Other Words remains one of only thirteen (at last count) feminist bookstores still in existence in North America. Feminist bookstores began flourishing in the early 1970s, with nearly two-hundred bookstores, gradually reducing to less than seventy around 2000. During the recent workshop there, after writing from prompts and considering the practices and principles, women shared what they wrote with someone sitting next to them and, later, with the woman on the other side. Then we opened the circle, each woman sharing something she felt comfortable reading that she had written with the whole circle.

This is the part I love the best, sharing the intimacy within our own journals with everyone present. I can see our hearts expanding as I sense compassion deepening through this magical, sacred work. I am grateful for this wonderful space that continues to nourish so many women throughout the years and decades. I am thrilled to be the inspiration for bringing these women together to write openly, honestly, authentically.

Envisioning Your Writing Alone Together Community

We cannot change the world alone. To heal ourselves, to restore the earth to life, to create the situations in which freedom can flourish, we must work together in groups.

—STARHAWK

Our dream is that you will receive the stories, words, ideas and tips within this book as inspiration and support for you to create a *Writing Alone Together* journalling circle of your own. May we all let the voice of the universe, the voice in each of us, move through us and out onto the page, alone and together, to serve the heart of transformation in our lives and in the world.

Final Journal Writing Prompt

Envision the kind of writing community you want to create, the ways you would like your writing to be in community, in connection with others. Create a vision of your Writing Alone Together community that would delight, inspire and serve you. Be bold and write from the heart. Trust yourself. Believe. Inspire. Write.

CIRCLES OF WOMEN
Wendy Judith Cutler (1992)

(Dedicated to all the Circles of Women Writing Everywhere
Together)

each time we pose
pen or pencil to paper
we connect with who we are   who we were   who we want
to be
we are circles of women
writing together
   apart
in dialogue
   alone
reaching for the depth
or surface brilliance
writing our lives authentically   intuitively   consciously
coming together
to read   to write   to share   to listen   to speak
knowing ourselves more
as we come to know others
creating a space
safe enough for our pain
and joy
our losses
and our resilience

write anything
about what?
write about anything
anything?
write about your hunger   cravings   desires
obsessions

I don't have any

think
write
let yourself go
go deeply
deny nothing

I used to write   a lot   stopped
someone read my words
my thoughts
I stopped writing
never wanted anyone else to know

tell the story of the betrayal   violation   criticism

there were other times
I became silent   ashamed   vulnerable

write it out
put it down
word by word
thought by thought

I'm scared
it's too painful
too boring
too wordy
too hard

breathe   stay calm   own your
feelings
acknowledge your experiences

confront your censors
go beyond your blocks
discover the source that fuels
your creativity   your words   your power

but that's frightening
I feel overwhelmed

just start writing
put it down
whatever comes
keep writing
don't stop

all right, here goes:
   I am a woman who...
      This is a day in the life of...
        An obsession of mine is...
          If I could change anything I'd...
write anything
from your heart   your body   your soul
write your pain
your joy
ambivalence
jealousy
write your regret
your truths
your dreams
your visions
write your lies
I am on a tropical island...
   I watch the waves...
      I am in the forest...
        I am alone in a cabin...
          I am on my bed...

I am in my favourite chair...

I am at my desk....

I am under a tree....

I am near the fire....

(in unison)
we write wherever we are

we write when we're overwhelmed

we write to clear our minds

we write to express our anger

we write to clarify our thoughts

we write when we're too tired to talk

we write to capture that exact feeling

we write to release our pain

we write to honour our truths

we write to connect ourselves to this circle

these circles of women writing

each time we pose pen or pencil to paper

(excerpted in *We'Moon 2011*)

Acknowledgments

Throughout this book-writing journey, we have been supported by many others: our loved ones and families, close friends and the many women we write and teach with in our communities on Salt Spring Island and around the world.

We offer our tremendous, unending gratitude:

- To women from all of our respective circles, classes and workshops over the years who have inspired and experienced the magic of *Writing Alone Together.*

- To our editor and sister-island writer, Lorraine Gane, who brought her poetic sensitivity to our nascent manuscript. Hers were the first eyes, ears and heart we trusted with our beloved book.

- To Mark Hand, whose artistry, design eloquence, patience and creative wizardry brought our manuscript to life.

- To Andrea Palframan, Corrie Hope Furst, Katharine Salzmann, Krystee Sidwell and Peter Allan for their generous and skilled reviewing, editing and commentary on first and subsequent drafts. Special thanks to Kerri Hampton for her concise copy-editing and review of the entire manuscript.

- To Derek Lundy for his enthusiasm and support of the original book proposal and his steady cheers along the way.

- To Adina Hildebrandt, Alda Blanes, Andrea Bass, Annie Mussey, Caffyn Kelley, Cheryl Cohen, Chris Lieschner, Christine Oades, Delaine Faulkner, Diana Morris, Elizabeth Toews Blakely, Emma-Louise Elsey, Gregory Watson, Johanna Brenner, Julia Prinselaar, Lana Lyons, Laura Schepps, Liesbeth Leatherbarrow, Linda Dobson, Linda Gilkeson, Linda Hilyer, Linda Kavelin Popov, Lisa Davila, Lisa Lipsett, Lynda Crawford, Lyra Hall, Marilyn Sronce, Marlyn Horsdal, Megan Wyckoff, Mia Korn, Nita Hertel, Pearl Gray, Peggy Williams, Premilla Pillay, Rebecca Shannon-Sharpe, Sarah Hook Nilsson, Sharon Bronstein, Trish Maddison, Trista Hendren and Vera Algoet for reading and listening to our words and providing support and constructive commentary along this journey of bringing our book into existence.

- To the writers who graciously devoted time to reading our manuscript and offered eloquent and appreciative words of praise: Kathleen Adams, Judith Arcana, Hannah Braime, Lucia Capacchione, Lorraine Gane, Ariel Gore, Carl Leggo, Tristine Rainer and Betsy Warland.

- To the writers who practice, promote and have written books about journal writing in all its varied forms, who have deeply inspired us in our passion for journal writing and have been absolutely necessary to the creation of this book.

- To the island we live on, Salt Spring, whose beauty and natural wonders nourish us and to all the creative, artistic, activist, earth-loving, caring communities of islanders who have supported and encouraged us.

- To our parents in love, birth and spirit: Selma Aronoff, Arnold Aronoff, Doug and Marion Monk, Diane Antkiw, Margaret and Harry Cutler.

Especially, we acknowledge our utmost gratitude to one another for our commitment, tenacity, resilience and understanding as sister journal writers, authors, colleagues and friends.

Congratulations! Cheers! Mazel Tov!
Wendy, Lynda and Ahava

Bibliography

Adams, Kathleen. *Journal to the Self: Twenty-Two Paths to Personal Growth*. New York: Warner Books, 1990.

Addonizio, Kim. *Ordinary Genius: A Guide for the Poet Within*. New York: W.W. Norton & Company, 2009.

Baldwin, Christina. *Calling the Circle*. Newberg, Oregon: Swan Raven & Company, 1994.

_____. *One to One: A New Updated Edition of the Classic Self-Understanding Through Journal Writing*. New York: M. Evans & Company, 1991.

_____. *Storycatcher: Making Sense of our Lives through the Power and Practice of Story*. Novato, California: New World Library, 2005.

Bass, Ellen. "The Meaning of 'Essay' is to Try." *Radical Teacher*, 1978.

Bolen, Jean Shinoda. *The Millionth Circle: How to Change Ourselves and the World*. Berkeley, California: Conari Press, 1999.

Braime, Hannah. *The Ultimate Guide to Journaling*, 2012.

Brown, Brene. *The Gift of Imperfection: Let Go of Who You Think You Are Supposed to Be and Embrace Who You Are*. Center City, Minnesota: Hazelden Publishing, 2010.

Cameron, Julia. *The Right to Write: An Invitation and Initiation into the Writing Life*. New York: Jeremy P. Tarcher, 1998.

Capacchione, Lucia. *The Creative Journal: The Art of Finding Yourself*. Athens, Ohio: Ohio University/Swallow Press, 1979 (Original Oversize Edition) & Franklin Lakes, New Jersey: The Career Press/New Page Books, 2002 (Second Edition).

Cerwinske, Laura. *Writing as a Healing Art: The Transforming Power of Self-Expression*. New York: Perigee, 1999.

Chambers, Cynthia. "On Taking My Own (Love) Medicine: Memory Work in Writing and Pedagogy." *Journal of Curriculum Theorizing*, 1998.

Cixous, Hélène. *"Coming to Writing" and Other Essays.* Cambridge, Massachusetts: Harvard University Press, 1991.

DeSalvo, Louise. *Writing As a Way of Healing: How Telling Our Stories Transforms Our Lives.* Boston, Massachusetts: Beacon Press, 1999.

Dowrick, Stephanie. *Creative Journal Writing: The Art and Heart of Reflection.* New York: Penguin Books, 2009.

Ferron. *Catching Holy: Poems 2006-2008.* Nemesis Publishing, 2008.

Fitzgerald, Maureen. *One Circle: Tapping the Power of Those Who Know You Best*, 2006.

Frost, Robert. "The Road Not Taken," *Mountain Interval.* New York: Henry Holt & Company, 1920.

Gane, Lorraine. *Unpublished Writing*, 2010.

Goldberg, Natalie. *Long Quiet Highway: Waking Up in America.* New York: Bantam Books, 1993.

_____. *Old Friend From Far Away: The Practice of Writing Memoir.* New York: Free Press, 2007.

Gore, Ariel. *How to Become a Famous Writer Before You're Dead.* New York: Three Rivers Press, 2007.

Griffin, Susan. *Made From This Earth: An Anthology of Writings.* New York: Harper & Row, 1982.

Hagen, Kay Leigh. *Internal Affairs: A Journalkeeping Workbook for Self-Intimacy.* San Francisco, California: Harper/San Francisco, 1992.

Hagberg, Janet O. *Wrestling With Your Angels: A Spiritual Journey to Great Writing.* Holsbrook, Massachusetts: Adams Publishing, 1995.

Hasebe-Ludt, Erica, Chambers, Cynthia M. and Leggo, Carl. *Life Writing and Literary Métissage as an Ethos for our Times*. New York: Peter Lang Publishing, 2009.

Herring, Laraine. *Writing Begins with the Breath: Embodying Your Authentic Voice*. Boston, Massachusetts: Shambhala Publications, 2007.

Hirshfield, Jane. *Nine Gates: Entering the Mind of Poetry*. New York: Harper Collins, 1997.

Holzer, Burghild Nina. *A Walk Between Heaven and Earth: A Personal Journal on Writing and the Creative Process*. New York: Bell Tower Press, 1994.

hooks, bell. *Remembered Rapture: The Writer at Work*. New York: Henry Holt & Company, 1999.

Lamott, Anne. *Bird by Bird: Some Instructions on Writing and Life*. New York: Anchor Books/Random House, 1994.

Lorde, Audre. *Sister/Outsider: Essays and Speeches*. New York: Crossing Press, 1984.

Metzger, Deena. *Writing for Your Life: A Guide and Companion to the Inner Worlds*. San Francisco, California: Harper/San Francisco, 1992.

Moore, Honor. "Polemic # 1," *New Women's Survival Sourcebook* (Susan Rennie, ed.). New York: Alfred A. Knopf, 1975.

Nin, Anaïs. in Rainer, Tristine. *The New. Diary*. Los Angeles, California: Jeremy P. Tarcher, Inc., 1978.

Piercy, Marge. *The Moon Is Always Female*. New York: Alfred A. Knopf, 1977.

Pod, Ai-Jen. "Interview on the Rights of Domestic Workers." *The Sun*, May 2013.

Progoff, Ira. *At a Journal Workshop: The Basic Text and Guide for Using the Intensive Journal Process*. New York: Dialogue House Library, 1975.

Rainer, Tristine. *The New Diary: How to Use a Journal for Self Guidance and Expanded Creativity.* Los Angeles, California: Jeremy P. Tarcher, Inc., 1978.

Reeves, Judy. *Writing Alone, Writing Together: A Guide for Writers and Writing Groups.* Novato, California: New World Library, 2002.

Richardson, Cheryl. *The Art of Extreme Self-Care: Transform Your Life One Month at a Time.* New York: Hay House, 2009.

Sher, Gail. *One Continuous Mistake: Four Noble Truths for Writers.* Arkana: Penguin Books, 1999.

Schneider, Pat. *The Writer as Artist: Writing Alone and Writing With Others.* New York: Oxford University Press, 2003.

Snow, Kimberley. *Writing Yourself Home: A Woman's Guided Journey to Self-Discovery.* Berkeley, California: Conari Press, 1989/1992.

Starhawk. *Dreaming the Dark: Magic, Sex and Politics.* Boston, Massachusetts: Beacon Press, 1982.

_____ . *Truth or Dare.* San Francisco, California: Harper & Row, 1987.

Thompson, Kate. *Therapeutic Journal Writing: An Introduction for Professionals.* London,UK: Jessica Kingsley Publishers, 2011.

Ueland, Brenda. *If You Want To Write: A Book about Art, Independence and Spirit.* Saint Paul, Minnesota: Graywolf Press, 1987 (Originally published by G. P. Putnam's Sons, 1938).

Vecchione, Patrice. *Writing and the Spiritual Life: Finding Your Voice by Looking Within.* New York: Contemporary Books, 2001.

Walker, Alice. *Sent By Earth: A Message from the Grandmother Spirit (after the attacks on the World Trade Center and Pentagon).* New York: Seven Stories Press, 2001.

Warland, Betsy. *Breathing the Page: Reading the Act of Writing.* Toronto: Cormorant Books, 2010.

Weingarten, Kathie. *Common Shock: Witnessing Violence Every Day. How We Are Harmed, How We Can Heal.* New York: New American Library, 2003.

Wheatley, Margaret. *Turning to One Another: Simple Conversations to Restore Hope to the Future.* San Francisco, California: Berrett-Koehler Publishers, 2002.

Winant, Fran. *Dyke Jacket: Poems and Songs.* New York: Violet Press, 1976.

Wise, Nina. *A Big New Free Happy Unusual Life: Self-Expression and Spiritual Practice for Those Who Have time for Neither.* New York: Broadway Books, 2002.

Woodman, Marion with Mellick, Jill. *Coming Home to Myself: Reflections for Nurturing a Woman's Body and Soul.* Berkeley, California: Conari Press, 1998.

Working with the Authors

WomenWriting with Wendy

WomenWriting inspires women to come together within circles of women to write and share our lives. In 1985, while teaching writing and women's studies in colleges and universities, I began offering journal writing workshops for women. We met in cafés and bookstores, retreat centres and conferences, offices and in my own home.

Since moving to Salt Spring Island, I have continued to manifest my dream of bringing women together to honour our truths, share our stories and deepen connections with our authentic selves. I teach memoir and journal writing workshops and classes and facilitate ongoing women's writing circles on Salt Spring Island, in Victoria, British Columbia and in the Pacific Northwest. I also occasionally have individual consultations with women.

My main intention is to create an environment, a sacred space, for women to feel safe, supported and nourished, because we can only be open, honest and vulnerable with ourselves when we feel safe and trusting. We draw from the "four practices" as I sensitively guide women into personal writing, deep listening, sharing and witnessing. The intimacy that is generated within these circles is profound and moving. This inspires ever-deepening connections and a sense of community through sharing our words, our hearts and our lives.

I am honoured to be part of these sacred, sensitive, trusting, courageous, wise and wondrous circles of women. I find that this magical experience occurs as women are drawn to these circles. I welcome you to join these circles of WomenWriting: Simply bring your self, a journal and the desire to write.

www.womenwritingwjc.wordpress.com

Wendy Judith Cutler, MA

Wendy Judith Cutler, M.A, is a teacher, writer and lesbian-feminist who has taught Women's Studies and Writing for more than thirty years. She has been involved in feminist, leftist, social justice and queer politics, community-building and culture for many decades. She was a contributor to *The Coming Out Stories,* is noted in *Feminists Who Changed America: 1963-1975,* and has had writings in numerous publications. Through WomenWriting, she facilitates journal writing and memoir workshops and circles. She relishes the opportunity to inspire women to honour the wisdom and power of their own words. Her memoir-in-progress is about lesbian feminism in the 1970s entitled *Memoir of an Undutiful Daughter.*

Writing for Wellness with Lynda

I am passionate about the healing and transformational power of writing—all writing—alone and together. Words can inspire, heal and transform us—writing can change the world.

A number of years ago, I created Life Source Writing™ —a five-step reflective journalling practice that integrates mindfulness, mind/body relaxation, expressive writing, inquiry and gratitude into a holistic and creative process which enhances emotional, physical, psychological and spiritual health. I am the founder of Creative Wellness —where writing, well-being and transformation meet. Through my workshops, virtual retreats, presentations, e-books, and coaching circles, I teach and support heart-centered women and men to go to the page to know, grow and care for themselves with Life Source Writing™.

As a Registered Social Worker and Life Coach, I also have specialized offerings for healthcare and helping professionals who want to use journalling and expressive writing for their own self-care, burnout prevention and personal growth, as well as within their healing work with clients or patients.

The core of my work in the world is to inspire and help people to live healthy and awakened lives through writing. Creative Wellness offers opportunities and tools to help women take time and space to write, reflect, listen within, deepen self-awareness and come home to the self through nourishing mind, body, heart and spirit—on and off the page.

You can access my free *Writing for Wellness Getting Started Guide,* which is filled with reflective journalling prompts and exercises to discover and nourish YOU.

www.creativewellnessworks.com

Lynda Monk, MSW, RSW, CPCC

Lynda Monk is a Registered Social Worker, Certified Life Coach and the founder of Creative Wellness—a journal coaching business where writing, well-being and transformation meet. She regularly inspires and guides helpers, healers, leaders and others to the page for self-care, stress relief, healing, growth and renewal. Lynda is the author of *Life Source Writing™: A Reflective Journaling Practice for Self-Discovery, Self-Care, Wellness & Creativity.* Her memoir-in-progress is currently called *Wild Abandon: An Adoptee's Memoir.*

Loving Inquiry with Ahava

As the founder and creative mentor at the Centre for Loving Inquiry, I help women gain the confidence and freedom to express their authentic creativity. Loving Inquiry is a practice that invites women to slow down and open to their inner wisdom by guiding them through metaphorical gates that encourage creative exploration and personal reflection. Each gate offers the opportunity to pause and notice their experience within the frame of a particular quality of awareness.

A Year to Love™ is a twelve-month mentoring program I facilitate with women to learn, grow and create together with the guidance of the gates. Biweekly gates (lessons), individual mentoring and monthly group retreats encourage artistic inquiry and expression. Using writing, collage, photography, video, dance, storytelling, music and other creative practices, each woman is empowered to tell her own stories and see herself in new ways. Through the support of this individual and collective creative practice, women overcome blocks that have kept them from fulfilling their artistic ambitions.

I am passionate about helping women love and care for themselves (and each other) as they follow their creative impulses, reclaim their joyful curiosity and develop their unique ways of being in the world. Loving Inquiry gives women the opportunity to exceed their perceived abilities, to risk and play in the unknown of their imaginations and to embrace the beauty and diversity of their voices and stories.

If you have a desire to love yourself and bring your artistic gifts and visions into the world, I invite you to walk with me through the Gates of Loving inquiry.

www.lovinginquiry.com

Ahava Shira, PhD

Ahava Shira, PhD, is a writer, performer, creative mentor and founder of the Centre for Loving Inquiry. Her innovative retreats and mentorship programs support women to develop their confidence, cultivate self-compassion and access their creative power. Author of *Weaving of My Being*, a poetry book and *Love is Like This*, a spoken word CD, Ahava has been courageously exploring her own artistic expression for two decades through her poetry and storytelling performances. Her memoir-in-progress about overcoming the limitations of a surgically fused spine is called *Curve*.